YOUR

SOUL

FOCUS

You Believe in the Afterlife, Don't You?

By

Annette Marinaccio

Inphinite Lumen, LLC

For information about special discounts for bulk purchase, please contact
Inphinite Lumen, LLC at: info@inphinitelumen.com

Printed in the United States of America
Library of Congress Control Number: 2020923511

ISBN: 978-1-7363751-5-0 (*paperback*)
ISBN: 978-1-7363751-0-5 (*e-book*)

This book is based on the author's recollection of true events that
transpired. Some names have been changed to protect the privacy of those
depicted.

"*Your Soul Focus* takes the reader on a journey of discovery into both why we're here and what comes next. Sharing truths about our existence garnered from years of personal exploration into the existence of life after bodily death. It will open your eyes and heart to the beautiful and continuing connections we share with those whom we loved who have crossed. This journey also offers insight into why we're here, and the beautiful roles we play in each other's lives."

- Laura Lynne Jackson, NY Times bestselling author of The Light Between Us and Signs: The Secret Language of the Universe

"*Your Soul Focus* is a compelling look at the extraordinary work of psychic phenomena."

- Robert E. Hansen, Psychic Medium, Author, Intuitive Counselor, and Public Speaker

"*Your Soul Focus* is a Truly Inspiring Journey of Spiritual Connections and Deep Understanding of "Signs from Above"!!! I recommend this book to anyone who knows or needs to know that love never dies! Annette Marinaccio's book is a true inspiration as to the understanding of how the soul reconnects to those they have touched here on earth. I found it to be Inspirational, Healing and a page turner!! A true testament that love never dies!!!"

- **Josephine Ghiringhelli,** Psychic Medium, Author, Intuitive Counselor, and Public Speaker

CONTENTS

DEDICATION

*This book is dedicated to my wonderful
family — forever…….and in particular, to my mother.
Her positive outlook on life is most
inspirational.*

INTRODUCTION

I had not desired to become an author. I am a successful healthcare executive and a Certified Public Accountant.

My mother-in-law led me on a path *after* she died to show me that there is an afterlife. I then spent many years learning everything that I was able to about the topic. I was most interested in how the afterlife relates to our lives.

I have accumulated a great deal of knowledge about the mysteries of life. I believe that I am one of the few people to have spent the time to accumulate this type of information without being able to validate anything spiritually myself. My hard wired, left side, analytical brain prevents this for me. I had to be convinced with visible, tangible, and otherwise unexplainable occurrences. I am able to connect the dots, so to speak, that spiritual people often take for granted and that non-spiritual people have a difficult time experiencing and believing.

My book unfolds my journey and what I have learned, chapter by chapter. It contains personal stories and anecdotes applicable to everyday life, entwined with the afterlife concepts that I have learned. I have been able to sort through an overwhelming amount of information to cull out the aspects that resonate with me. After understanding that the afterlife is existent, I learned how intricate and extensive our souls and our journeys are. It is absolutely fascinating!

In many instances, I have found myself in the position of being able to convey what I have learned to help others to understand something that seems elusive to them. I see that my knowledge and communication have been helpful to others during times of grief.

It is for that reason, that I became intent on writing this book with the possibility that it just may help someone during their time of grief, need, or curiosity. It is a spiritual book that is written in a practical way. It is an easy read with some significant takeaways. Knowledge is the antidote to fear. It is as simple and as complex as that.

PROLOGUE

"You believe in the afterlife, don't you?," my friend said incredulously. I don't know. I was not sure if I believed. I had not thought about it. I had pondered it years ago when I was younger, but I became busy with working and raising a family, so it simply was not something I had time to think about or to discover.

I am not terribly intuitive. The side of my brain which is the strongest is the analytical side, the left side. I excelled and loved math growing up. I still love numbers. I never tapped into or had the interest to tap into my spiritual side until now.

CHAPTER 1

The Pom - Pom Story

It was Wednesday morning, October 25th of 2006. I was enjoying breakfast with my beautiful 13-year-old daughter, Diana, before she headed off to school and I headed off to work. We just had a very emotional weekend saying our final goodbyes to my mother-in-law. I know many people have, well, I guess you might say interesting relationships with their mothers-in-law, but mine was not like that at all. When she died at the young age of 68, I told my husband, we lost the sweetest member of his family. He was not insulted. He agreed.

At the kitchen table that following Wednesday morning, my daughter decided to let me in on a most interesting story from her previous day at school. She said, in an innocent and matter-of-fact way, "I got a sign from Grandma yesterday."

As my children were growing up, we had never really spoken about the afterlife or receiving signs from deceased loved ones. I had always been matter-of-fact about death when the topic would arise from time to time. I recall once before the era of cell phones and GPS, I was driving my mother and my two young children somewhere, and I got quite lost. I was outwardly panicking. My son said, "Are we going to die, Mom?" I quickly answered, "Yes, of course, we're going to die. Everyone dies, but I don't think it's going to be today." I was surprised by the question, but was more focused on figuring out how to find our way. That became my response every time after that when my children asked about death. "Yes, of course we'll die, but I don't think today's the day." I was pretty matter-of-fact about the uncomfortable topic.

We had buried my mother-in-law on a Saturday and the following Wednesday, Diana continued to tell me that in her art class, her assignment was to make a textured card. She decided to make a Christmas card with green and red pom-poms. She was in a relatively small class with about a dozen students. Each student had their own table to stand and work at, as well as their own supplies. The common supplies were stored in a closet in the art room. Diana told me that she went to the art room closet and took the pom-pom container back to her desk. It was a large container with pom-poms of many colors and sizes. She took 11 green and 11 red ones out to make her card. I don't know why 11 of each color. I did not ask why. I was just listening. She let me know that she recounted the pom-poms and left them out on her table before carrying the container back to the closet across the room.

Diana is a bright, strong girl. She is visionary, creative, and detail-oriented. It would be just like her to double-check that she had counted correctly. Then, when she returned to her desk after putting away the container, she found a surprise! There were her 11 green and 11 red ones, along with one white one and one lavender one. I listened intently, thinking clearly that is not possible. She must be thinking that she saw them, but they could not have really been there if she had not put them there, could they? She then asked if I wanted to see them. Of course, I said yes. I was skeptical that she would have them, but she ran up to her bedroom and, sure enough, came down with a lavender and a white pom-pom. I was surprised.

I asked her how they got there. Her eyes lit up. She exclaimed, "I don't know! I wish I had seen it." I could see she was genuinely curious about their presence and that she had tried to answer that very question herself. Diana is quite practical. She had worked through all of the possibilities in her mind. She concluded that they either floated there through the air, or they just appeared. Either way, she wished she had seen what occurred. She said there was nobody around her desk who could have put them there. I asked her what she made of this. She said, "Grandma must be thanking me for the balloons." The pom-poms were the exact shades as the gravesite balloons we had released on the prior Saturday for my mother-in-law. I did not know what to make of it.

I was fascinated by this story. I was telling it to everyone that I encountered over the subsequent days and weeks, both my personal and my professional friends. Something of this nature is not a typical conversation, especially in an office. However, I was trying to make some sense of it. Most people were shocked or did not believe me. I guess they thought that Diana had concocted a coping mechanism and placed the pom-poms there herself. I must admit that I also had thought of that possibility. But she was so sincere and innocent. She was also so curious about how they appeared. She had thought through other people placing them there, which she said was not possible. She thought through her placing them there by mistake, which she also said was not possible, since she double-checked before bringing the container back to the closet. She worked through all the possibilities and concluded her grandmother had somehow made them appear. Fascinating.

A month or so later, I was telling one friend in particular. Donna was a close neighbor and dear friend. We first met years earlier, when we both moved into our neighborhood at the same time. Her two children were about the same ages as my two children. Our husbands also got along. We all instantly connected. Although we had socialized on many occasions, the topic of the afterlife had not been discussed. Now I was standing with her and conveying the pom-pom story. Her reaction shocked me. Instead of Donna being surprised about the unaccounted for appearance of the pom-poms, she was surprised that I was even a bit doubtful about the afterlife. She said incredulously, "Well, you believe in the afterlife, don't you?" And so, my journey began.

CHAPTER 2

A Mysterious Tune

My journey actually began several years prior to the pom-pom story, however I had not realized it at the time it was occurring. When my daughter, Diana, was young, like many children, she loved to sing. She would sing all different kinds of songs, some that she learned from tapes, some she learned from children's television shows and some she learned from our family. She was so cute while she would sing her tunes, capturing our attention. When Diana was about two and a half years old, she began to sing a new song. I had not heard her sing it before. It was a catchy tune and she would sing it intermittently over the upcoming months. "I come to falcinella, remember my so." It doesn't mean anything in particular in English. And I'm not sure that I am spelling it correctly, but phonetically, that is how it sounded to me. I must admit that I found it particularly interesting since my grandparents' last name was Falcinelli. Not exactly in the song, but falcinella sounds awfully close to Falcinelli, doesn't it?

Diana had never met my grandparents. Although I was very close to my grandmother, she had died years before my precious children were born. I was so distraught when my grandmother died. I recall being inconsolable at the wake and burial. When she was alive, I spent a great deal of time with her, helping run her errands and visiting her all the time. She was a widow for decades. As she became older, my mother wanted my grandmother to live closer to us, so my grandmother moved. This relocation made it quite easy for me to stop by and visit. We would sit and watch television together in her apartment. If I think about it, I can actually smell her tomato sauce, filled with parmesan cheese, as she would make delicious pasta and meatballs for me many times during my visits.

When Diana started singing this new tune, I was curious. Diana was too young, at two years old, for us to have spoken about her great grandparents. We had not even had pictures of them around the house. To me, I thought, hmm, these words sound very similar to, "I'm Grandma Falcinelli, remember my soul." But I discounted that because it seemed unfathomable. How could my daughter come across those words??

One summer day, when Diana sang the song, I asked her where she had learned it. I was a little afraid but mostly curious as to her answer. She said very matter-of-factly, "Grandma taught it to me." Hmm, I slowly posed the next obvious question, "Which Grandma?" She hesitated while she thought about it, and then she replied, 'Grandma Margarita.' That was my mother. Whew, I was relieved, since an otherworldly answer would have unnerved me.

My mother was very close to my children. While I went to work, I would bring my children to my parents' home. My parents spent many days caring for my children. The relationship that developed is an extremely close and loving one. This tune was not something that I'd ever heard my mother sing or hum; however, I guessed it would be possible that my mother had a few songs up her sleeve that she taught to my children and that I had never heard of. My parents did a lot of things with my children that seemed new and different to me.

Since the song was an intermittent event, I kept forgetting to ask my mother about it. However, during that Christmas holiday season, my parents were visiting and I remembered to ask my daughter to sing the song. She looked at my mother, her grandma Margarita, and she sang the tune, 'I come to falcinella, remember my so.'

I turned to my mother to ask if she had taught it to her. My mother shook her head. She had not. Hmm, that was curious. I then asked my daughter again, who taught that song to you. Diana looked at my mother in a confused way. I could tell that she wanted to say Grandma Margarita, but that she also thought that it was not Grandma Margarita who taught it to her. After a minute or so of confusion, she announced, "Grandma Lucille."

That was my husband's mother, also Diana's grandmother. We are a very close family, so my daughter was very close to Ralph's family too. Now, I was a bit more curious, though, because Diana was confused about how she learned this tune. I certainly had not heard my mother-in-law singing this tune. And the word falcinella would not be one that my mother-in-law would be singing about. The Falcinelli surname is on my side of the family.

My daughter turned three that February. She continued to sing the song intermittently. In the spring, I finally remembered to ask my mother-in-law about the song. I asked Diana to sing the song.

I asked my mother-in-law. "Did you teach her that song?" No. Now, I was perplexed. Diana was so young and innocent. She was also a clear-minded child. It did not fit to me that this little tune had seemingly confused her so. The fact that falcinella sounded so much like my mother's maiden name was now starting to strike me as poignant in some way.

I asked Diana again, who taught her the song. She looked at my mother-in-law. Diana seemed so confused. My daughter was struggling and trying to figure out who taught her this tune. She then said in a bit of an animated, almost upset way, as if I was pushing too much in terms of wanting to know, "It wasn't Grandma Lucille. It's my other grandmother. The one who puts me to sleep at night."

I was now very shocked. I know that I read a book to Diana every night before leaving her to fall asleep. So, which grandmother could be putting her to sleep? I was anxious about this answer. What is she talking about? I then asked my last question on the subject because this all seemed so confusing to me also, "Which grandmother puts you to sleep at night?" She said, "The one who sits on my bed."

She was no longer matter-of-fact about who taught this tune to her, as she had been a few months earlier when declaring it was my mother, her Grandma Margarita. I could see she was confused by the whole thing. She was sure that the person who taught her the song was her grandmother. But she also had learned in her young three years of age that she had two grandmothers - Grandma

Margarita and Grandma Lucille. And the person who taught her the song did not seem to be either of them.

I was a bit amazed at this, of course. I had no idea what to make of it. What could I say? I left it at that. I was confused, and so was Diana.

My daughter had been singing this tune off and on for about ten months by this time. Could my grandmother be in touch with my daughter? It seemed fictional and impossible. But I tucked it in the back of my mind, as something fantastical that I could not explain.

CHAPTER 3

The First Medium

About a year after my daughter was singing her mysterious tunes and still before the pom-pom story, I was driving to work one morning, and there was an advertisement on the radio. A famous medium named Suzane Northrop was coming to Long Island. She was performing and doing readings for a large group audience. Suzane was an internationally acclaimed psychic medium. She had written a best-selling book. She travelled all over the world selling out venues where she would deliver messages to family members from their deceased loved ones. When the tickets for her local venue went up for sale, they sold out within a matter of days. I was curious, so I purchased three tickets to take my mother and mother-in-law to the show.

When the evening of the event arrived, the three of us entered the ballroom of a local hotel. We were three of about a hundred people seated in rows. It was a varied grouping of people sitting lecture style on chairs that would typically surround a dinner table. I noticed that there were mostly women with some men. They were mostly adults, with some younger adults.

Suzane started by explaining a bit about her gift. She let us know how she would deliver messages from our deceased loved ones. She said that she sees our deceased loved ones as if they are on various levels, sort of from top or above our head to bottom, or waist level. For instance, someone coming through at a higher level would be a parent, aunt or uncle's age group. Someone coming through at a lower level, would be a child, niece or nephew's age group. Someone coming through at our shoulder level would be a brother, sister, friend, or cousin. She answered some specific questions about some of what she had learned from the other side. I listened to her introduction with extreme skepticism. She seemed kind enough and possibly sincere. However, it seemed a bit overreaching to me. I was interested but viewed it more like a magic show of some sort.

The woman seated next to me was alone. While Suzane moved around the room, she landed on this woman. Suzane had a message from the woman's deceased mother. Suzane proceeded to convey precise details that seemed impossible for this Suzane to know about. She conveyed that her mother passed of an illness at her home. She said that the woman seated next to me had cared for her mother until the end. Suzane said that the woman's mother was thanking her profusely for caring for her and for telling her it was ok for her mother to die at her end of life. The woman was quiet. She kept nodding her head in agreement, as her eyes were welling up with tears. I concluded that although this woman seemed authentic, she must be planted there so that the audience would believe that Suzane had some ability to bring through deceased loved ones. After Suzane left and went on to convey messages to others, the woman next to me started sobbing. I gave her some tissues to wipe her tears. I thought it was great acting on her part. She did seem quite genuine.

Suzane read about a dozen audience members. All were as moved as the woman seated next to me. People were passing tissues around. Some people were sobbing and some were laughing at various stories about their deceased loved ones. I was surprised but thought it was possible that she knew these people in advance. I thought maybe they flew internationally from show to show with Suzane as part of the crew or act. I thought that maybe she used our credit card or check information to garner the necessary information in some manner to put on this exciting show.

The internet was not as pervasive at that time, but there must have been some way for her to gather this background information. Although obtaining specific details about deceased loved ones' personality traits or specific occurrences while people died did not seem like information that could be obtained from credit card information. The messages seemed detailed and specific enough; however, the possibility that our deceased loved ones were conveying them, seemed unbelievable to me.

She did say one thing that I hung onto, though. She noted that children choose their parents before they come to earth. I liked that thought. I don't know if I believed it, but I liked it. It came in quite handy for me throughout my children's youth. As they complained about me, I would say, "Well, you chose me." For example, one time, my son compared me to his friend's mother, saying something along the lines of, "Kevin's mother doesn't make him eat breakfast every morning." It was handy for me to have the comeback, "Well, then I don't understand why you selected me instead of Kevin's mom?" As you can see, this concept is beneficial. At that time, I was not convinced that it was true, but it could be true, and it worked for me.

CHAPTER 4

Ten Dollars

My Uncle Charlie was my father's older brother. They did everything together. They owned a dry cleaning business and worked together every day. They bought the same cars as one another and they lived blocks away from each other. My Uncle Charlie was five years older than my father. My uncle is very outgoing and a strong personality type. My father is more quiet and a homebody type. They got along perfectly. They saw one another almost every single day. Even when one was not headed to their dry cleaning business for the day, my uncle would bring breakfast to my father and they would enjoy their meal together before starting their day. Their deep bond and love for one another was obvious. When my father won $7,500 in Atlantic City once, he split it with my uncle without hesitation, although my uncle was not even there. They were best of friends their entire lives. My father and my uncle were the opposite in terms of their personalities, but they loved each other fiercely.

I was also very close to my uncle, since we enjoyed many family functions and activities together during my childhood. I have such fond memories of him and the pool parties that he would host at his house. My Uncle Charlie died in April of 2000. We were all devastated. I recall screaming when I found out that he had died. We were all inconsolable at the wake and funeral. He had suffered a stroke a few years earlier, but he had recovered, so we had not been expecting his sudden death.

In our church, there was a section on the side with candles that one could pay to have lighted for a deceased or ailing loved one. It cost $100 and the church would light it for six months in honor of the specific person.

After his death, in November of 2000, I walked to the rectory of our church to pay to have a candle lit in his name. I wanted a candle lit for him during the upcoming holiday season. After parking my car and as I was walking toward the rectory, I found a ten-dollar bill on the ground folded very neatly and tightly. It was lying on the grass at the edge of the sidewalk on the walkway leading up to the rectory. I had never found a ten-dollar bill on the ground before. I have found pennies, nickels, dimes, maybe even a one-dollar bill, but a ten-dollar bill, that was quite a surprise. I picked it up and kept it. I still have it. I thought it was interesting that I found it on the grounds of the rectory on the way to have a candle lit for my uncle. I went in and paid for the candle. A few days later, the church contacted me. They let me know that they would be returning my $100 donation. It turned out that my father's sister, my Aunt Mary, had already paid to have a candle lit in my Uncle Charlie's honor for the holiday season. Interesting, I thought. I had more money than I had prior to going there by the ten dollars that I had found, and there was a candle lighted for my uncle.

CHAPTER 5

Wait, What, Mom?

I was walking back and forth while I spoke on the telephone with my mother late on a Sunday evening at the end of September of 2005. It was just a catch-up call to check in on my parents. I was in the habit of visiting my parents or at least calling weekly. My parents lived in the same town, so I would see them often and we spoke often also. I would see them as they cared for my school age children, on the days that I went to work. That particular evening, we spoke about my week and the family, nothing specifically. The room that I was sitting in while on the telephone was dark. I had not bothered to turn on the lights. It was just a telephone conversation. I did not need lights on for that. It was a Sunday night, and I was focused on catching up and then getting myself ready for work the following day.

At the end of the half hour or so conversation, my mother added one last update. Her annual mammogram had yielded a positive result. Her physician had arranged for an ultrasound as the next step. It was scheduled in a month from today. What? A positive mammogram? Are you sure? A follow-up test a month from today? Isn't that a long time between a positive mammogram and the next test, the ultrasound? Yes, that is far too long. My nightcap conversation had somehow turned into a nightmarish kind of ordeal. Why had my mother waited until the end of the telephone call to let me in on this significant situation?

I spent the next day arranging for an emergency ultrasound for my mother. We were not waiting for a month. I work in the healthcare industry, so I was able to get an appointment reasonably quickly with a top New York doctor.

My mother had a crappy insurance plan. My sister spent the next several weeks navigating with the insurance plan's representatives to move the payment for the next month's appointment that we had canceled to the next day provider that we went to.

We took her for the ultrasound. Since we have no history of breast cancer in our family, we were hopeful that this more involved test would yield nothing of interest. To our dismay, we were wrong. The ultrasound was also suspicious, so the physician took a biopsy on the spot. Then, we waited for the results. It was less than a week since our Sunday night call. What a whirlwind week. We were struggling to understand what was occurring. We know that is how it happens sometimes, an innocuous occurrence turns into a life changing event. We know that nobody is really prepared for that type of unexpected situation. We know this happens all the time to people. However we were caught off guard nonetheless.

My mother had been in a minor single-car accident back in the spring. She was pulling the car forward into a parking spot and hit the curb quite hard. Her body pressed into the steering wheel. She was convinced that the incident is what was now causing this issue with her breast. She was also afraid that it had caused cancer. She said that when she was younger, she had heard that accidents like that could cause cancer. She knew a young girl that was struck by a tennis ball and got cancer in the spot where the tennis ball had injured her. I reassured her that this was an old wives' tale. Bruises due to impact could not turn cancerous, could they? My mother had been a young girl in the 1930's when the girl was hurt by the tennis ball. Certainly science has proven that is not the cause of cancer all these years later, right?

It was an early October Saturday at the end of our difficult week and I was running errands. I passed a bookstore that was going out of business. All the books were $1 each. I stopped in and bought some young adult books. I did not spend a lot of time reading their prologues. For $1 each, I was not concerned about wasting money. I just bought a couple of books that had catchy covers and titles for my two children.

When I returned home later that day, I gave the books to my lovely 12-year-old daughter and ten-year-old son. Diana loved to read and began to read the book that evening. After a couple of chapters of the first book, she came out of her room and was quite upset. "Why would you get me this book? It is about a girl whose grandmother has breast cancer? It's horrible." I apologized and told her not to read any more of it. I had not read the content. I had just picked up the book. What are the chances? Ugh.

I knew that she and my son, Joseph, had likely overheard my discussions with my husband as I arranged the various medical tests for my mother, but we had not discussed anything with our children yet. We did not want to burden them unnecessarily. With no history of breast cancer in our family, we were hopeful that the biopsy would be fine. However it was obvious that they had heard our whispering discussions.

About five days after the biopsy, the breast radiologist called me. She said the results of the biopsy were inconclusive and that the cells were quite unusual. She said that they were going to send the tissue sample to a very specialized pathologist in Manhattan. OK, so we waited again, but this time, with more concern.

Columbus Day was a sunny one that year, and I had the day off from work. My children were home from school. I decided to take my daughter out east for a shopping trip to the outlets. It was early in the afternoon, and we had our arms full of shopping treasures. I had just opened the car door to place them inside. My daughter was getting into the car. Ironically, it was decent timing for me to be able to take a call. My phone rang. It was the radiologist involved in my mother's case. I took the call outside of the car while my daughter settled inside.

There are just some moments in life that indeed are life-changing. Their life-changing attributes become crystal clear as time marches on. This was one of those moments. She said, "I am so sorry, Annette. Your mom has cancer." I could no longer stand outside the car. I could no longer stand. I did not want my daughter to have to deal with this, but I had to sit immediately. I sat in the car.

The doctor went on to say that it was an extremely rare and aggressive form of cancer, spindle cell carcinoma. My

33

mother would need an appointment scheduled with a surgeon immediately. I thanked the physician and hung up the phone. Now what? My car was full of new clothes and accessories, my heart was racing, and my 12-year-old daughter was full of concern. She was asking me what was going on with her grandmother. We were about 45 minutes from our home and my hometown, which is where my parents also lived. I gathered my jumbled emotions and started heading back to Farmingdale. I explained the situation as best I could to my daughter. I reassured her that we would seek the highest level of care for her grandmother.

I decided to pick up a pizza, bring my daughter along, and head straight to my parents' house. We arrived, ate the pizza, and when we were finishing, I let them know that I had heard from Dr. Roberts. The results had come in from the specialized pathologist. It was cancer. My mother remained relatively calm, but I could feel the shock and fear emanating from her core. I am confident that she had been preparing herself for this possible news for the last week or so, but hearing it was so challenging.

I don't know if it was better to have the news coming from me, her oldest daughter, or coming from a physician. I think it was better that I delivered the news and that it was in her kitchen. It was the kitchen that I grew up in. It was the kitchen that she worked so diligently to fill with memories of excellent food, smells, and meals throughout so many decades. It was the most comfortable place to receive the most uncomfortable news.

We called my sister and brother to let them know the bad news. The whole family focused on what to do next. The answer to that was to make an appointment with a breast surgeon. I worked on that the next day and I was able to schedule an appointment for a few days after that.

Throughout the next days and weeks, we got a crash course about breast cancer, medications, reactions, and various treatments. When a tumor is localized, it is typically Stage One. In my mother's case, the tumor was localized, but quite large and such an aggressive form of a cell type that it was categorized as Stage Two. Most cancers have four stages. So, Stage Two meant it had not spread, so that was good at least. Both of my mother's parents had died of cancer. My grandfather died of lung cancer in his late 60's, but he smoked, so it was attributed to that. My grandmother died of thyroid cancer in her early 70's. We were very much attuned to the fact that my mother at 75 years of age had outlived both of her parents.

Our next year was filled with my mother's breast surgery, then very aggressive chemotherapy, followed by harsh radiation treatments every day for five weeks. There were numerous doctors' visits, insurance company negotiations, more medical jargon than I would ever have thought that I could understand, and such a variety of medicines and drugs. My mother endured days of nausea, extreme fatigue, and suffering. The days turned into weeks and turned into months. The various side effects of these treatments were prescriptive. Her hair fell out on cue. She would question whether the treatment was worse than the disease. We explained that we had no choice but to press forward with the various treatments. We were determined to do anything possible to kill these cancer cells, as any family would be in these circumstances. All told, it took a year of long, challenging days.

CHAPTER 6

Wait, What? Again?

We also lived quite close to my in-laws. They lived about two towns away from us. So, we were able to visit them quite often. They are very family oriented and so are we. My mother-in-law had felt a bit ill for years. The doctors never found anything precisely wrong with her. Her blood sugar was a little high, maybe pre-diabetes. She frequented doctors because she often did not feel quite right. Her urine was typically a bit off, but blood tests were always inconclusive. We were all accustomed to her seeing doctors. She seemed healthy to us, but she was still going to her doctors, having blood tests done, ultrasounds, urine tests, gastrointestinal tests, and yet all of these tests yielded no diagnosis. Her appetite was okay and she looked good. This cycle of doctors' appointments and various tests went on for years.

The day after my mother's breast cancer diagnosis, my husband called me at work. He rarely called me during the workday, so I suspected something was amiss. He reminded me that my mother-in-law had revisited her doctors and had tests done again, but this time there was a difference. This time her ultrasound showed a couple of spots on her liver that made the radiologist hesitate and ask for a CAT scan. He said that they were likely lipomas, fatty deposits on the liver that occur with age, but he wanted to be sure. My husband asked me to arrange for the CAT scan test to be done as soon as possible at one of the medical offices where I worked. I did.

My mother-in-law and father-in-law both came into the office early the following week. Although I was not ordinarily working in that particular medical office, I greeted them there. When my mother-in-law went in for the CAT scan, I went behind the scenes. Two great radiologists were working that morning. I was friendly and comfortable with both of them.

I went into one of their offices while my mother-in-law was being scanned in another room, as I knew they would view the images in real-time, and they would let me know what they saw. We waited for a few minutes. The images came onto Dr. Maggio's video monitors. He scrolled and scrolled. He looked and looked. In a matter of minutes, almost moments, he said, "I want Dr. Cavit to see these also." I immediately got nervous. Dr. Maggio was an excellent radiologist. It took him such a short amount of time to say that he wanted another radiologist to look at my mother-in-law's images. He said that he was not confident about what he was looking at. I knew that he was quite experienced. It did not make sense to me that he was unsure in such a quick amount of time.

We walked into Dr. Cavit's office right next door. They pulled the door shut and called up the images on Dr. Cavit's video monitors. The three of us were in the darkened office, which is optimal for a radiologist to read images to arrive at a diagnosis. Dr. Cavit scanned through the images on his oversized computer monitors. He looked at the images one at a time. Unlike Dr. Maggio who made a quick decision to obtain Dr. Cavit's thoughts, Dr. Cavit was spending more time than I would have thought he would need to decipher these images. After what seemed like an eternity, he finally said, "I am so sorry, Annette." Now I was confused and starting to go numb. I had no idea what this even meant. I questioned, "I don't understand? What is it?" It is pancreatic cancer, and it has spread.

I fell to the floor, business suit and all. What? How? I did not ask if they were sure. It was clear to me that they were convinced — both of them. I was immediately overcome with a feeling of nausea. I could not think straight. I did not know what to do. Do I call my husband? Do I go out to the waiting room and say something to my in-laws? What are the very next steps with horrific news like that??

I took the advice of the radiologists that I worked with. They said that I should not be the one to deliver this news. They said that an experienced physician would know how to explain it and how to answer any questions. The physician would be able to strategize on next steps. They also said that I should tell my husband before my in-laws found out. I took that advice, which felt cowardly to me. I waited until I gathered the strength even to call my husband.

I let the office staff inform my in-laws that they were done with the exam and should head back to their internal medicine physician's office, as they would send the reports to them on the same day. I did not even go out to see them off or to say goodbye. I was uncomfortable not saying goodbye to them, however I was afraid that they would detect my fear and that I would have conveyed this horrific news to them before I was even able to let my husband know. I called my husband. He left work immediately and began his one hour plus commute to his parents' home.

Over the next few days, we soaked in as much as we could about pancreatic cancer. We just completed our crash course about breast cancer a few days earlier, as my mother had just been diagnosed, so we had enough foundation to understand that this was horrible. Pancreatic cancer is basically incurable if it has spread. We had just educated my children about the stages of cancer. We had conveyed that there is hope for someone with an earlier stage of cancer. My mother's cancer was Stage Two. My mother-in-law's cancer was Stage Four. My kids broke down. We were all devastated.

Our next year was filled with my mother-in-law's pancreatic cancer treatments. It entailed very aggressive chemotherapy and an alternative therapy also. We had an already planned surprise trip to Disney World to give to my parents-in-law as a Christmas gift. We planned it with my sister-in-law and her family. We had the trip planned for February of the following year. We had all scheduled the vacation days at our respective employers. We had airline tickets. We had the hotel reservations. We were all looking forward to surprising my in-laws on Christmas Day. Now with this horrendous news, we realized that this life change would change everything for our family. It would change our fun plans. It would change our daily lives. It would change everything. I recall asking the oncologist when the treatments would end, would it be four weeks, six weeks? I was wondering if we might still be able to take our trip after her course of treatments. The oncologist conveyed that with pancreatic cancer; the treatments won't likely end. They will go on until the patient cannot take it anymore. What??! That's horrible.

And that is what happened. The next year was spent with both my mother and mother-in-law fighting for their lives. It was a whirlwind of doctors' visits, medicines, and insurance companies. When we would visit my mother, she would ask, "How's Lucille?" The answer was, "Not great." When we would visit my mother-in-law, she would ask, "How's Margarita?" The answer was the same, "Not great."

CHAPTER 7

Reassurance

After about nine months, my mother-in-law took a turn for the worse. She was deteriorating and was hospitalized. A few days after my mother-in-law was admitted to the hospital, my daughter came into the kitchen to let me know me that my grandmother, her great grandmother, was in her dream last night. Hmm, interesting. I did not know what to make of what my daughter was telling me. Neither my grandmother, nor any other deceased person, had ever visited me in my dreams. But my daughter was only 12 years old and why would she make this up? I listened carefully. She said that my grandmother said to her, "Don't worry about your other grandmother. We will take care of her over here."

I just listened, thinking maybe she was making this up to cope with the circumstances. I then recalled her song from a decade earlier, when she was so young. Back then she was too young to understand much about her deceased great grandmother. But now at 12, she was aware of our family history and had seen pictures of my grandmother. So, I asked the next question, "Has Grandma Falcinelli ever come to you before in your dreams?" She thought for a minute and then said, "Yes" in a fascinated, animated way. Diana let me know that my grandmother had come to her twice before.

I held my breath and listened. Twice before? I had not brought up to Diana the catchy tune from a decade earlier. Could there be an ongoing relationship between my deceased grandmother and my daughter? I was thinking that she would convey the stories from when she was two years old. But I was wrong. Instead, she shared a totally different story. It was equally as amazing. And Diana was so in awe of it herself, that it was impossible for me not to believe her.

Diana said that several years earlier, my grandmother had come to visit Diana in her dream. Diana continued to tell me that my grandmother had been trying to convey something at that time to Diana. My grandmother had building blocks with letters of the alphabet on each one. She was trying to spell out her message. But the blocks would topple, and Diana could not understand them. In addition, Diana got scared and woke up. She vowed to herself that if my grandmother ever came to visit in her dreams again — she would not get afraid; she would stay asleep and listen to the whole message. Well, that was fascinating to me. There would be no reason for Diana to make up this story when there isn't even a message involved.

Then Diana continued. She let me know that my grandmother did visit in Diana's dreams again. It was a few years after that first dream visit and a couple of months ago. It occurred on the day of Joseph's confirmation. Joseph is my son and Diana's brother. So that would have been a weekday in May of the year that we were in. Diana said that she had a dream that we were at my parents' house, and their answering machine was flashing. My mother pressed the button to hear the message. It was my grandmother. She said, 'Hi Margarita. It is mom. I wanted to say congratulations on Joseph's confirmation.' That was it. I thought to myself — that's interesting. Maybe since my daughter was afraid a couple of years earlier when my grandmother visited with the building blocks, my grandmother figured to have the person and the setting in the dream be someone and somewhere that my daughter knew and would be comfortable with. So, she had my mother play an answering machine while still getting her message across. So it was only my grandmother's voice in the dream. The visible aspects of the dream were my mother and my mother's house, a place and person that Diana was supremely comfortable with.

Now, here we were a couple of months after that dream, standing in our kitchen. My mother-in-law had taken a distinct turn for the worse, and Diana was conveying these fantastical stories to me. My grandmother was coming to her in her dreams to offer comfort. I am uncertain which seemed more unbelievable — that these dreams really occurred or that my daughter made these stories up so readily. Either option seemed almost impossible to me. I did, however, have the scenes from when my daughter was two years old playing in the back of my mind. My daughter had not added those to her accounts, but I could not help but recall them. My fascination continued.

Over the next several months, there were intermittent hospital visits and emergency surgeries to try to keep my mother-in-law alive. It was horrible. When there was no hope left, she died in the palliative care wing of a local hospital with her immediate family at her side, my father-in-law, sister-in-law, and my husband. The wake and funeral were devastating. I was inconsolable. We all were. Her four beautiful grandchildren let go of white and lavender balloons at her gravesite after the graveside prayer at her burial. It was just one year after her diagnosis, and she was gone. From vibrant to gone in one year. It was too much for us to comprehend. But we had no option. We had to confront it. It was real. And it was raw.

CHAPTER 8

The Pom - Pom Summary

Four mornings after we buried my mother-in-law, I was at the breakfast table with my beautiful daughter before she would head off to school and me to work. This morning was the fateful morning when my daughter decided to let me in on her interesting events from her previous day at school. She said, in an innocent and matter-of-fact way, "I got a sign from Grandma yesterday." She continued to tell me that in her art class, her assignment was to make a textured card. She conveyed her story about the container from the art room supply closet. She told me about the red and green pom-poms. She ran to her room to show me the white and lavender pom-poms that had materialized in her art class. She said, "Grandma must be thanking me for the balloons."

CHAPTER 9

You Believe in the Afterlife, Don't You?

Donna had been my neighbor for ten years at this point. She was a working wife and mother like I was. Our husbands also became friends, so we would try to spend time together whenever we could. Sometimes it was just a stop for a conversation when one of us was passing the other on the street. Other times it would be an evening out for dinner. We had spoken so many times over the ten years, but somehow the topic of death or life after death had not been raised.

About a month after my mother-in-law died, I saw Donna on our street before we would both head off to work, and after we had set our children on their busses to head to school. I walked over to let her know about my recent most incredulous story. The pom-pom story. She smiled and nodded throughout. She waited for the point where I embrace the everlasting soul, spirit concept as if I had understood and embraced it all along. She paused as if, of course, we all know that we live on past death. But I was not at that stage. I was just trying to understand how my daughter found these pom-poms.

Donna listened to my story. I ended my story with total bewilderment on my part. She just stared at me for a bit. I could see that she was sure there would be more to my story. But there was no more. She asked me incredulously, "You believe in the afterlife, don't you?" I said I don't know. I never really thought about it. She was stunned at my answer. Here we were sort of close and yet, she had not known that I was unaware of the afterlife! Of course, we live on after death! She was so matter-of-fact about it that it shocked me.

Donna then conveyed several stories and examples in her past to let me in on this best-kept secret. Although it was not a secret really, because she just assumed that I was aware all along. She said that she had gone to several psychic mediums and had connected with her deceased loved ones many times. She told me that she frequents a particular medium, based on Long Island, visiting several times after her father died. Donna said that when she needs advice, she goes and asks the medium to tap into her father's energy to advise her.

Donna gave me an example of when her family was trying to determine whether to sell her mother's house after her father died. While there, her father's spirit promptly came through. He not only advised them to sell the house, but he also advised them where to buy his widow's next residence. How is this possible? I listened skeptically. I trust Donna. She is a bright, practical friend, but I was not sure that this was possible. I paid extra attention to this perplexing story.

Donna told me that the medium, Josephine Ghiringhelli, said things that Donna was unaware of. Josephine mentioned a miscarriage from Donna's father's family. Donna had not known about it, but her mother confirmed it afterwards. Donna also said that she went there while she was pregnant with her first child years ago for advice.

Donna's mother initially did not want to go to any medium because she felt like it was a form of devil worship. Donna's husband accompanied her one time, but he was uncomfortable. Although Donna had gone to several local mediums, she recommended Josephine G. because she was terrific and she had a wonderfully compassionate way about her. Donna had gone for several private readings with her. The concept of the afterlife was a large part of Donna's life. I was amazed and of course, couldn't keep my mind off of this during my drive to work.

Donna's testimonial is on Josephine's website. I recalled hearing Josephine at some point in the distant past on a local radio show on my way to work. I was fascinated at the time, but not enough to pursue anything. At that time, it was merely interesting to me. I viewed it as some type of magic show. I tucked this conversation with Donna neatly in my head, figuring that I would explore it at a later date.

Over the next few months, I continued to tell the marvelous pom-pom story to people. Some people grabbed the story and added their own experiences of metaphysical possibilities. Some people would shut it down and not want to speak any further. It is a very personal topic, so I approached it with caution.

I also continued to play some of what Donna said over in my head. I tried to poke holes in her perspectives. However, that was difficult to do because I had not experienced it firsthand. It came down to a matter of my trusting that she was sincere and that she had no reason to develop a sophisticated coping mechanism to deal with her father's passing.

I also could not help but think back to when my daughter was two and three years old. Her comments about the song taught to her by the grandmother that put her to sleep at night. I did not know what to make of this all. It would be comforting to believe that somehow our loved ones don't just rest in peace somewhere disconnected from us. It would be comforting to think that our loved ones continue to exist in some manner after they die. It would be comforting to believe that I would not just disappear when it was my time to pass, and that would be the end of it. It would be comforting to believe instead that I would continue in some capacity. However, I never really spent a lot of time thinking about it. And without being able to validate it — it did not seem like anything that I would be comfortable believing anyway.

We move forward, even though the grief envelops us at times that we don't expect.

CHAPTER 10

Out to Dinner

My family and I were getting into our new routine. We were grieving over the significant loss of my mother-in-law. We were learning to combine that harsh feeling with living our daily routines. We were grieving. Grief is an interesting feeling. Most of us grieve over the past quite often.

For example, I wish my children were young again. I get quite sad to think that they will never be three or four years old again. That time is gone. The interesting thing is that my children don't even remember what they were like at those ages. It was like those cute times were there for my enjoyment, instead of for theirs. One can get lost in the longing for the past. The only thing that helps me to work through and come out of that type of grief is the fact that I can see and speak with my children now as adults.

It is difficult for me to explain, but grief for the loss of a loved one is similar, except it is much more challenging to work through because we are not able to see and speak with them later today or tomorrow or next week or ever. The feeling of sadness about a past time in our lives and our not being able to have that ever again for me is similar to the sadness about losing a loved one. The difference is that I can think of spending happier times in the present and future with those people that were part of my past, and that are also still alive. I cannot have that with someone who has died.

As humans, we really do not have any foolproof coping mechanism to overcome grief. We only have the ability to compartmentalize the sad feelings and thoughts within ourselves, as we try to navigate our daily routines. We individually develop the ability to live our daily lives despite the fact that our loved one is no longer present to converse with, to see and to hold. We move forward, even though the grief envelops us at times that we don't expect it to. It comes and goes like waves in an ocean. They crash closer together when we are near the shore and they are further apart from one another when we go further out to sea. The waves are just as intense, but more intermittent when out at sea. It is like this with grief, as time marches on, the waves become farther apart from one another. But when they do occur, they are just as intense as they were initially after our loved one crossed over. And they never disappear completely, nor would we want them to.

Our new normal meant that we could no longer spend time with my mother-in-law. We invited my widowed father-in-law to dinner every weekend that we could. I would typically make a lovely Sunday dinner for all of us, or we would all go out to dinner on a Saturday evening.

A month or so after my friend, Donna, told me about her experiences with mediums, my husband, son, recently widowed father-in-law, and I went out to eat at a local restaurant on our hometown Main St. It was early in December, so quite chilly. Once we got settled in, I happened to notice that one of the large front windows that we were seated near had a full-length poster facing the street. Although we were on the inside, I could see through it enough to see the pictures and wording.

Lo and behold, this restaurant was having a dinner and medium show on a Sunday evening at the end of the upcoming April. And who was the star of the show, none other than — the medium – Josephine G.! Geez, my friend had just filled me in on Josephine G. and now this. I could not believe this string of coincidental events. My mother-in-law passes, my daughter gets the pom-poms, I tell Donna the story, she raves about Josephine G, and now Josephine

G is coming to a restaurant within walking distance of my home that I happen to go out to eat at. What an unlikely coincidence. We had been to this restaurant often enough, and they had never hosted this type of event. I wanted to go.

When I got home, I reached out to Donna and asked if she wanted to go. She said absolutely, yes. I asked a third friend to join us also. I called the restaurant and made the reservations myself. "Annette – a party of three," I asked about payment. They said I would pay at the event — cash or credit card — either would be fine. Hmm, so I provided no information other than my first name and how many people were in my group.

CHAPTER 11

The Second Medium

On the last Sunday evening in April of 2007, Donna, our friend, Susan and I drove to the restaurant in our town. We were looking forward to dinner and the show with Josephine G. We checked in, 'Annette - a party of three.' No further information was requested or given. The hostess led us to our table. It was a comfortable booth along the wall. There were about 100 guests seated for dinner and the show with Josephine G. There were booths along the walls and tables in the center of the room. There was an assortment of people attending. Some were old, some were young, some were with their family members, and some were there with their friends. There were men and women. Some tables had two people and some had eight or so people.

After everyone enjoyed our dinners and when our desserts were in front of us, a fellow came out and introduced Josephine. He mentioned her local radio appearances, classes that she taught, and he mentioned her ability to connect with our deceased loved ones. Josephine promptly came out. She had a microphone allowing all to hear her. She began her show with a brief introduction saying that she would be conducting readings and that we should all listen carefully as our loved ones would speak to us through her. She said it was important that we validate our loved ones' messages as they were conveyed. She said that the validations that we provided would encourage our deceased loved ones to convey more and more. Josephine explained how she would see information conveyed to her by our deceased loved ones. I listened intently, but skeptically. Josephine seemed very sweet, so not someone I thought would have a sophisticated mechanism for deceit. However, if she were not deceiving us all, then this would make what she was saying authentic, which seemed even crazier.

Josephine started on the other side of the room from where we were seated. She was bringing through a deceased police officer or firefighter. There was a family of about six people there. They were connecting to these messages and validating them. I thought to myself that they might have known Josephine G. They were likely planted there to allow her to start her show with what appeared to be a big hit.

Then, she moved across the room with purpose and stood right next to our table. She promptly said that she had someone named Lucille here. Lucille is my mother-in-law's name. I could not move, let alone raise my hand. My head was spinning. Did my friend, Donna, convey this to Josephine? My friend would not set me up behind my back. Could Josephine have used my reservation information to determine my mother-in-law's first name? I do not think that was possible either. I said nothing. I was petrified. Josephine went on saying, "Whose Lucille, Lucy, someone with an 'L'?" I was rationalizing that she was not exactly at our table, although she was standing right in front of us. I was hoping that this message may be for the adjacent table. My friend, Donna, was kicking me under our table, trying to get me to take the microphone. She already understood the afterlife. She had no doubt that this was my deceased mother-in-law. Donna was glaring at me. "That's your mother-in-law, take the microphone," she was wording to me across the table. I could not 'take the microphone'. I froze.

Finally, the woman at the table next to us raised her hand. She said that her name was Elizabeth. She pointed out that her name had an "L" in it. Josephine conceded and handed her the microphone. Whew, I was so relieved. I was hoping that maybe these messages would be for Elizabeth and not for me. Josephine went on to tell Elizabeth that she could see that she was going to Europe in a few months. Oh no - I had in fact booked a trip to Italy in a few months. Elizabeth told Josephine that she was not going to Europe but that she had gone to Florida several months ago. After some time, Josephine left Elizabeth and went to read others, connecting with all. Josephine was leaving people stunned and in tears of bittersweet joy. My friend Donna was upset with me for not taking the microphone. But I could not have. The whole thing made no sense to me.

About 20 minutes later, Josephine came right back to our table. She said that she had a soul there who had died of something like stomach cancer. She said that the woman was holding her stomach in pain. Nobody raised their hand. Again, Donna kicked me under the table and said, "Take the microphone." I hesitatingly raised my hand. Josephine said, "Oh yes — she is telling me to go to the woman with the dark hair and blue shirt." Yes, - that described me — but that was plain to see.

Josephine continued with my reading. She let me know that she had a mother figure present who had passed with incredible pain to the stomach area. She had passed from an illness like stomach cancer, but not stomach cancer. Yes, I let Josephine know that my mother-in-law did pass from pancreatic cancer. Josephine said that my mother-in-law told her that I was like a daughter to her. Yes, I agreed that we were very close. Josephine continued and said that my mother-in-law was with Teresa. My mother-in-law's mother-in-law was Teresa. They were not that close to one another, however, Ralph's grandmother Teresa was the only one of his grandparents that I had met. Then came the question that turned my life inside out. "Who is Margarita?" I said, "What?" Josephine repeated, "Who is Margarita?" I said, "Margarita is my mother." Josephine asked, "Is she still here?" Before I could answer, she answered the question herself. "I see that Margarita is still here." I then agreed, "Yes." She said, "Oh – because your mother-in-law is saying, 'Say hello to Margarita for me.'"

During the year that my mother was treated for her cancer and my mother-in-law was being treated and dying — every time I visited my mother-in-law, she would always ask how my mother was doing, and she would say, "Say hello to Margarita for me." There was simply no way that Josephine could know that, let alone tie me with my married name, which Josephine did not even know, to my mother's first name. Also, the name "Margarita' is an uncommon name. And Josephine had picked up on my mother-in-law's name, "Lucille," as well as my mother's name, "Margarita". I was done. I was shocked for a moment, but then like a bolt of lightning, I could see immediately that this was not a hoax. I could not explain this away. It was real and happening to me. My mother-in-law was working hard to get me to this place of knowledge, for which I am so grateful.

I took the reins from my mother-in-law. She had done all of this. She had indeed placed the pom-poms on my daughter's desk. My mother-in-law had selected Josephine G. My mother-in-law made sure that I saw Donna to convey to her my pom-pom story. My mother-in-law made sure that Donna could tell me her stories, including her positive endorsement about Josephine. My mother-in-law made sure that I went out to eat at the local restaurant to see the Josephine G. poster to get me to this evening to open my eyes and the eyes of my/her loved ones.

Josephine G. asked if it had taken an unusually long time to select her tombstone. It had not taken too long, but my sister-in-law had agonized and frequented the vendor every weekend day and then some. She and my father-in-law had many discussions about it. It was quite intense for several months. My husband was also involved. Josephine asked if we had something engraved on the tombstone that was difficult to have engraved. My sister wanted a butterfly on the tombstone. The company that sold the tombstone to my in-laws did say that engraving a butterfly would be a freehand design and may not look good. But my sister-in-law was persistent. They engraved it and it looks perfect. My mother-in-law said that she appreciated all of their efforts and she even commented on how she loved the butterfly that my sister-in-law decided to have engraved on the tombstone. My mother-in-law gave her sign of approval!

Josephine then asked if my father-in-law had sold his house. I said no. She said that they were showing her a real estate transaction that took years to consummate. She again questioned if he had finally sold his house. Again, I said no. She asked if I possibly might not know if he had sold his house. I said that I would know. He had not sold his house. I realized at this point that Josephine had not asked when my mother-in-law passed. Josephine did not know that it was six months prior. It may have been six years prior for all she knew. She continued asking if he was planning on selling it. Again, I said no. Her continued line of questioning was very interesting to me because if she were fake, she would have jumped to something else in front of all of these people, but she was so persistent about this real estate sale. I felt a bit embarrassed for her, since it seemed to be misinformation and she had a large audience all witnessing this mistake. She kept saying that she saw a real estate transaction that took several years to consummate, but that had just recently occurred. She eventually stopped and went on to say that my mother-in-law was all about family, which was right, and that she came to me through birds, which I love.

Josephine read several others and then she closed the evening with a group meditation. She asked us to close our eyes and to place an object in the hand of our loved one in our mind's eye. I opened my mother-in-law's hand in my mind's eye and I placed an orange monarch butterfly in her palm. Then, Josephine said that our loved one would show us that object back within two weeks. Once I realized what we were doing, I thought to myself that there is no way that my mother-in-law can show me a butterfly now. We were in April. Butterflies come around in the summer, not the spring. So, I moved the butterfly over in her hand in my mind's eye, and I placed a quarter beside it, hedging my bet. Josephine said we would each see our item show up in our life in the upcoming two weeks. We should watch for them. "Really?" I thought. There is a science to this? Again, this seemed incredulous.

In the car on the way home, I was replaying in my mind every minute of the evening that I could recall. I realized that a month earlier, my father had finally sold the real estate of the business that he co-owned with my Uncle

Charlie after seven years of trying to sell it. Since Josephine had initially asked if my mother-in-law was my mother, saying that she was a 'mother figure.' Well, then, although she was asking about my father-in-law and the real estate, maybe the topic was really about my father. Josephine had said that deceased loved ones come through as levels above, below or to the side of the sitter. Mothers, fathers, mothers-in-law and fathers-in-law would all be the same generation level above me.

I realized that the real estate transaction that she referred to may very well have been the business real estate that my father finally sold after years of trying. Maybe the part of the reading that I thought was a miss, was not really a miss after all. Maybe she was so persistent because it is real. Although I was concerned for her mistake and others may have wished that she would move on from her misinformation, Josephine persisted because someone on the other side was insisting on having their message conveyed. I thought that might have been my Uncle Charlie trying to come through.

When I arrived home that Sunday evening, it was quite late. My husband was already in bed. I could not sleep, of course. My head was replaying every detail of the evening. I quietly asked if he was awake. He mumbled something. I then could not contain myself. I woke him and proceeded to tell him every detail about the evening. He was actively listening. He was also fascinated, although I could tell that he was thinking to himself that I might be exaggerating or something. I knew that I was not though. He knew that I am a practical, skeptical and realistic person. So he was a bit curious now also. What could this all mean? Now we were both in wonderment.

CHAPTER 12

We Need Milk

The day following the restaurant and Josephine G. medium event was a Monday. I had to work late that evening. I stopped at Waldbaum's, a local grocery store, on my way home to get milk. It was about 9 pm. I knew the store's layout since I shopped there quite often. The milk was located in the back of the store. I could walk down any aisle to get to the back, so it did not matter which aisle I chose. I decided to walk down only one aisle since I only needed one thing. I did not even take a shopping cart with me. I decided to walk down the iced tea aisle since we could use that in the house also. Ok, I will pick up two items.

While walking down the aisle to the milk, I found a neatly, tightly folded ten-dollar bill right there lying on the floor, out in the open. Nobody was around. I immediately remembered the neatly folded ten-dollar bill that I had found seven years earlier on the way to the rectory to light a candle for my Uncle Charlie. I was surprised. A ten-dollar bill isn't an ordinary item to find on the ground, which is why I recalled it instantly. And now I found two in my life. One seven years ago on the way to the rectory while going to have a candle lit for my uncle and now a second one in the grocery store the day after the medium show, which I was thinking that my uncle had been trying to come through at. What are the chances of that? Very remote I would think. Could this be a confirmation from him that my thought about it being him trying to come through the night before was likely accurate? My head was starting to spin with this possibility.

The following Sunday, one week after the restaurant and medium event, I was reading the Sunday newspaper. The Life section had a feature article about butterflies on Long Island. When I opened to the article on page 16, there was a half-page color picture of an orange monarch butterfly! I immediately remembered the orange monarch butterfly that I had placed in my mother-in-law's hand in my mind's eye at the event a week prior. How is this possible? How would my deceased mother-in-law be able to effect a newspaper that I would read? I kept that newspaper in guess I doubted it in the future. Only in case of what, I don't know, but I did keep it anyway.

After work on the Wednesday of that week, I decided to grill steaks for my children, my parents, and myself on our backyard grill. As they all settled in the house, I walked out onto the porch and down the steps to the grill. It was a chilly early day in May, so it was the first time this season that we were going into the backyard to use the grill. When I came back into the house with the dish of cooked steaks, I found an Indiana quarter on the second step of the porch! It was right where I was going to step, shiny and bright. I thought it was neat that it had the word Diana in it, my daughter's name. I have no idea how it got there. I had not seen it the several times I had gone in and out while I had the steaks cooking on the grill. I remembered the quarter, the second object that I had placed in my mother-in-law's hand in my mind's eye. The event had been a week and a half prior. Josephine had said that we would be shown our signs within two weeks. That is exactly what occurred, with not one, but with both of my signs. Now I was starting to become unnerved. I knew that my friend, Donna, would have gladly accepted these signs; however, I was still struggling with what it all meant.

These happenings, the ten-dollar bill in Waldbaum's, the half-page color picture of the orange monarch butterfly, and the Indiana (even down to the detail of having the word "Diana" in it) quarter were life-changing. They were within one and a half weeks of Josephine G's readings. These three signs were the first personal signs with which I connected. I was beginning to understand.

CHAPTER 13

Filomena

I had to make sure that my husband experienced what I had just experienced. After all, it was his mother who was guiding me down this path. I had to share it with Ralph.

Ralph and I met twenty years earlier at work. We immediately hit it off and were attracted to one another. We began dating, got engaged two years after that, and were married one year afterward. Our life together had its ups and downs, like most couples. I know that many people say that opposites attract. That is not the case with Ralph and me. We are very similar. We are both strong personality types. We are both extremely hard-working, loyal, and have similar family values. We even have similar tastes in terms of food and activities. We have one area where we are opposites, which I had not understood until later in our marriage. He is an extrovert and I am an introvert. We are both quite social, so I always assumed that we were both extroverts. However I learned that the difference is not whether one is social or not, it is where one draws their daily energy from. He draws his from people and I draw mine from solitude. So, although we both love being around people and meeting people, we are opposite with respect to that trait. At any rate, we are both determined and stubborn people, so we stayed the course and carried on past any difficulties during our married lives, focusing on the joyous times. And thankfully, there were enough happy times to carry us across the challenges.

Ralph's family consists of his parents, his sister, and him. They are all very close to one another, so once we were a couple and eventually a family, we visited them quite often. I enjoyed the many afternoons and evenings spent with Ralph's family. They are loving and they totally welcomed me. So, it was easy for me to embrace them as my family also. When Ralph's mother took ill, Ralph spent as much time as possible with her. He would come home after a long day of work and a long commute and head to his mother's house to spend time with her before coming home and going to sleep and doing it all again the next day. It was difficult not having him home during those weeks and months, but I was careful not to convey that. I knew that his mother's days were, unfortunately for all of us, limited. It was very emotional to see her deteriorate and then ultimately to see her pass. This recent turn of events where she seemed to be communicating to me from the beyond appeared sort of encouraging. Did it seem like maybe she was still around?

I had begun to almost stalk Josephine G. by peeking at her website constantly. I saw that she had these small group readings in her office. There was an upcoming reading for a group of ten people in her office in Selden, so I registered Ralph and myself. Annette, a party of two. The reading took place in the living room of her office in a small run-down house on a main road. Her office inside of this house was surprisingly lovely and warm, decorated with angels and candles. There were only nine people there, so we lucked out a bit. The chances of a slightly longer reading were better since we were two out of the nine, instead of two out of ten, people. The session was 1 ½ hours, and everyone was guaranteed a mini reading.

The very first person to come through was my Uncle Charlie. He must have been waiting for this since he was cut off a few months earlier. Josephine said that there was a father figure near me. I knew it was my Uncle Charlie, so I just said that I think it's my uncle. Josephine asked if I suffer from headaches. I said no, although I had one today for some unknown reason. Earlier that afternoon, I had taken a Tylenol, which is rare for me. Josephine said that my uncle had mentioned to her about the headache, so that is why she asked me. It was interesting to me that he knew about that, since it was just something that happened to me earlier that day. Josephine also asked if he worked with chemicals because he was making her smell burning rubber. I said yes — he was a dry cleaner with my father!

Josephine then said that my Uncle Charlie was bringing through my grandfather, whose name started with a "V." I said, yes, my grandpa Vincenzo, thinking of my mother's father. She questioned whether he was on my mother's or father's side of the family. I replied on my mother's side. She seemed confused but carried on with the messages. She said that my grandfather was there with my uncle. I figured out that was likely why she was confused. This grandfather is on my mother's side of my family, while my uncle is on my father's side. We were a close family, so I was not surprised. She conveyed that they were showing her the Three Stooges. She said that they were both showing her a television that they were watching. I almost fell off my chair. I was so intent on it being my mother's father, Vincenzo, that I had not remembered at that moment that my father's father was my grandpa Vito. He was also a "V" name. My grandpa Vito loved to watch the Three Stooges, Laurel and Hardy, and I Love Lucy. It was not my grandpa Vincenzo at all. It was my Grandpa Vito! I immediately had fond memories of him sitting in our home with his leg up over the arm of the chair, watching these funny shows, and laughing out loud.

Some books that I have read afterward have said that naysayers would say that a psychic medium is merely reading your mind. That, in and of itself, would be amazing to me. But here, she could not even be doing that because I was thinking of the wrong person until she pointed out the specific television show.

Now, I was becoming more convinced. Here was my Uncle Charlie coming through to let me know it was him and to let me know he had survived "death." Josephine continued, saying that he wanted me to see that he was still actively involved by loving and protecting me and that he is always with me. This information was quite thrilling.

Then, while my head was still spinning with exhilaration and my husband was a bit shocked also, my mother-in-law came through! Josephine asked if Ralph was born in November. Yes, he was. Then she asked if he worked with numbers. Yes, he does. Josephine asked if his mother was on the other side. Yes, she is. Josephine then said that my mother-in-law said she was very proud of Ralph. She went on to say that there was another mother figure with his mother. A figure a level above his mother, so a grandmother. And then it happened.

Maybe for everyone, but certainly for me and now for Ralph, there is that one line or instance that defies logic. It opens the door to the possibility of life continuing after death because there is almost no explanation other than my deceased loved one is bringing this information through. Josephine asked, "Who's Phil, Phyllis – wait a minute — who's Filomena?" Are you kidding? What an unbelievably uncommon name. And yes, it is Ralph's grandmother's name, his mother's mother. Ralph and I were amazed. What a unique name. There is no way that Josephine could have guessed that out of thin air and no way she would have been able to Google it!

Josephine then added that my mother-in-law was thanking us for giving a young girl the earrings. Oh – that's right. Before my mother-in-law passed, she had given Ralph opal earrings that Ralph had given to his mother as a gift decades ago. She wanted to give them to my daughter for Christmas, which she realized would be a holiday after she passed. Here we were in Josephine's home office and my mother-in-law was thanking Ralph for making sure the earrings were given to her granddaughter, our daughter. It seemed that my mother-in-law had let us know it was her. She was providing these messages to Josephine. She was also letting us know that she had survived "death." She was letting us know that she was still actively loving and protecting us. She was letting us know that she was still with us.

There again were many "hits" that evening. When we returned home, Ralph and I were talking. I could not tell if he was as amazed as I was. I was also still sort of trying to make sense of it all. I tried to downplay the evening. I focused on the more skeptical side of my nature. I thought it would provide the opportunity for Ralph to say what he felt without being concerned about bursting my growing bubble. I said, "I think that there were many items that could have applied to any of the nine of us there. Do you think that?" He replied, "Not Filomena, not Filomena." He was right — how could she have pegged that rare name. There was no denying it for him and me. There were no explanations that we could think of other than the possibility of an afterlife and that my mother-in-law was giving Josephine that information. Although some of the messages could have applied to others in the group, other messages could not apply to anyone other than to the person it was being delivered to.

CHAPTER 14

The Third Medium

I was in awe and disbelief about these events. I now had a repertoire of stories that I was telling so many people. I had the pom-pom story, this coincidental series of events that led me to the mini reading by Josephine G., my Uncle Charlie bringing through my Grandpa Vito, even though I did not realize it was him, the butterfly sign, the ten-dollar-bills, and now these readings with Ralph.

My stories fascinated one professional friend in particular. Karen was a banker. She is well-loved and well-respected in the Long Island business community. Karen and I developed an easy professional and, eventually, personal friendship. She is an active person. One thing that Karen did was to volunteer a great deal of her time to the American Heart Association. After I had shared my experiences with her, she coincidentally happened to be attending an American Heart Association fundraiser that had a Chinese Auction. A Chinese Auction is an event where you purchase raffle tickets, then you select the specific prize you'd like to win, and you place your tickets in the basket for that particular prize. Then if your ticket is selected, you win that individual prize. One of the items was a set of two tickets to a group reading by a local psychic medium named Robert Hansen. She put her raffle tickets in there and said to her husband that if she won — she would give the tickets to me. She won.

She tried to give me the tickets after telling me her story. I told her I could not take them. My recent events had me thinking that there may be some validity to the topic of an afterlife. I let her know that if I am on to something here, then the tickets that she just won are like gold. I could not take them from her. She insisted. I decided to take the tickets and to take her as my guest.

It was a Wednesday evening after work in July when Karen and I attended the group reading in Robert's studio. There were about 50 people present, sitting in chairs that were arranged in an auditorium style. Robert arrived and explained how he would proceed to channel the spirits of our deceased loved ones through for us. And that is what he seemingly continued to do.

It was even more mind-blowing for me than Josephine's evening had been. I was becoming more open to the possibility that the people being read may not have been planted there. These readings may legitimately be coming from the deceased loved ones of those that were read. We were not read, but I learned a great deal. I started to see the different styles of mediums. Robert read about seven people that evening. He was more in-depth than Josephine, more specific, but his personality was also far more direct.

Josephine had started her group sessions with overall messages. She said that she asked the souls not to communicate any negative items to her, so she never really delivered anything negative to the sitters. Robert Hansen was different. He was very precise. Although Robert handled the messages delicately, the messages were more direct. He seemed to have September 11th victims/heroes come through first. Robert was quite graphic as to how they died. For one family, in particular, he explained exactly how the September 11th victim died. Robert stated that a beam fell on his chest and that the man could not breathe. He said he smelled the smoke. His family had not known precisely how their loved one's actual death occurred. Now they had this level of detail.

There was also a father and his teenage daughter in the audience. A second daughter of the man, and therefore sister of the girl in the audience, had died as a teenager several years earlier. Robert asked if the living sister was having current heart problems, and if she was seeing doctors. The father and sister answered yes. Robert said, "Go to another doctor. You are seeing the wrong doctor. You are not getting the care you need. You should be going to the Boston Children's Hospital as soon as you can." Robert's messages were particular and direct.

He also read the women right next to Karen and me. This woman was in such tears of joy. I could see that this medium's style was very different. It did not matter to me, though. I was not looking for anything from anyone in particular in terms of receiving a message from my deceased loved ones. I was not grieving for anyone, as many other attendees were. I was trying to figure this all out. The different perspective that this medium provided was interesting to me.

Karen and I were in awe. Since that day, Karen has become one of the individuals that I share my afterlife and spirituality stories with. She has become a dear friend and confidante.

CHAPTER 15

Support Is Important

Now that I had experienced these awesome adventures and had exposed my husband and a good friend to them, I could see how powerful this was. All three of us were unaware that this was even possible. And now, we were all open to it. I was fascinated. I wanted to share this important information with everyone that I knew and especially with everyone that I loved. If this was real, which it certainly seemed to be, then everyone should be viewing their life and their death very differently. In addition, I wanted to absorb and learn as much as I possibly could about this all. After all, in the words of the late, great Ralph Waldo Emerson, "Knowledge is the antidote to fear."

It was only months since my mother-in-law died, but she was busily exposing me to this crucial, life-changing information.

My next venture was to take my sister-in-law, Laura, and my father-in-law to a session of ten people in Josephine's office in Selden. Once again, my mother-in-law came through for us all. This time, Josephine was not as specific as the past two times — but again, she said some positive things that allowed the three of us to know that my mother-in-law and my Uncle Charlie were genuinely communicating with Josephine. My mother-in-law said that she was with my father-in-law when he read the newspaper at his kitchen table every day, which he did. My mother-in-law said how he had not moved her clothes yet and how they were all still in the same places that they were in when she was alive, which was accurate. She also said that my father-in-law should continue to live across the street from my sister-in-law, as she needed him. He does live across the street from her. It was certainly good advice all around. Josephine conveyed yet another series of pieces of information that was valuable and uplifting for all of us.

Next, I took my parents to a session of Josephine's. My Uncle Charlie and my Grandpa Vito came through for my father in a big way. Josephine conveyed to us that my uncle was standing in his army uniform, right near my father. Josephine could see that he was stationed in either Germany or Italy. Yes, — he was stationed in Germany. Josephine asked if my father was born in

September – as they were showing Josephine the number '9.' Yes, — my father's birthday is September 9th. My grandmother on my mother's side came through for my mother, also. The bottom line is now my father had gone from someone who a week ago would have said — "When you're dead — you're dead," to someone who now felt that was not the case. That transformation is invaluable. I was so happy to be showing my family that it seems to me that we carry on in some form, in some place, after we supposedly die. How fascinating!

CHAPTER 16

Mediums and Visits

I continued to read any materials that I could find and to attend medium and metaphysical events. I learned that the mediums sometimes get floods of information that they are deciphering and translating for the sitter. They are doing this while simultaneously listening to the tidbits that the sitter is conveying to them by either indicating that they can relate to this information or that the information doesn't resonate with them. The medium often has several souls speaking to them at the same time so that the messages may get a bit jumbled. Also, the souls may show them pictures that mean something to the medium, so it's not always verbal telepathy. It can also be visual, a scent, or a feeling. I was starting to understand how these readings progressed. And why some may be a little off.

I learned that mediums had varying levels of proficiency. It has something to do with a scientific aspect called frequencies, which I don't understand. A human's frequency of energy is quite slow and dull. Once we cross over, the souls' frequencies are quite rapid. To communicate, a soul has to lower their frequency, and a human has to raise theirs. We can increase our frequency through meditation. When we sleep, our frequency elevates also. It seems counterintuitive to me because I think of these restful states as lowering our energy level. Yet somehow, our frequencies rise during those relaxing activities. That is what occurs.

It is, therefore, easier for our deceased loved ones to enter our minds when we are asleep. Many people have had these dream visits. The people dreaming are often uncertain if what they experienced was a real visit from their loved one or if it was a dream. A dream is very different from a visit. Dreams become fuzzy in our memories over time, while visits are crystal clear and stay that way over time. Visits often have meticulous details. Your loved one will make sure that you wake up immediately after the visit so that you will remember it. Visits are a bit more real than a dream, although they still may have some nonsensical aspects to them. You may recall some precise details, like the color of clothes, the feeling of the touch of a hand, or the look of an eye. Those details that we remember don't typically fade over time.

Those details stay with one for days, weeks, and months. We can conjure them up quite vividly. It is also true that our loved ones and our Spirit Guides will help us work through issues in our dreams while we sleep. The saying, "Let me sleep on it" can be helpful advice.

Of interest, even the souls of our living relatives or friends can visit with us while we sleep. During those sleeping stages, souls can convene and help each other to learn and to grow. My father, who is alive, once visited me during my sleep to convey an interesting soul concept to me. He was outside of his house. He was about 75 years old in my dream, although in life, he was actually 90 years old. In this visit, he held his backyard gate open for me and he motioned for me to walk from his backyard to his front yard. When I walked through the gate, I was quite surprised. I found a second younger version of my father. He was about 55 years old. I exclaimed, "How can you do this? You're able to have more than one version of yourself?" My 75-year-old father nodded yes.

My father was showing me the infinite power of our souls. There were no words exchanged, yet we had this conversation. I awoke immediately afterwards. The visit was quite vivid and memorable. The 75-year-old version of my father was wearing a grey button down shirt tucked into his trousers. The 55-year-old version of my father was wearing a long sleeved multi-colored polo shirt over more casual pants. My father was reminding me that one doesn't have to be deceased to visit someone in their sleep.

Several days later, I mentioned this visit to my adult daughter. She was so relieved that souls of living relatives can visit in our dreams. Apparently my father had visited my daughter in her dream during the same evening that he had visited me. In my daughter's dream, my father was his current age of 90 years old. He kissed my daughter's hand, which he often does in real life. She immediately woke up. She knew it was a visit, but was confused because he is still living on earth.

Then we realized that he had visited both of us during the same evening, showing us that a soul can be in so many places at the same time. I had been surprised that my father could be both 75 years old and 55 years old at once. Now he showed me that he was able to be 90 years old at the same time as those earlier ages also. While we sleep, souls find it easier to visit and to convey things that are important things to us.

Mediums are more able to move their brainwaves into these higher frequencies, even while they are awake. In many cases, it seems to be an inherited feature, like artistic ability. It runs in individual families. There have been controlled scientific studies that monitor the medium's brain waves during meditation and during a reading. During both of those times, their brain waves are noted as being very different from when their brain waves are not meditating or doing a reading.

The various ways that mediums hear from our loved ones are called the Clairs. Clairvoyant is when they have a clear vision. Clairaudient is when they have a clear hearing. Clairsentient is when they experience sensations or feelings. Clairempathetic is when a medium experiences clear emotions from a soul. Clairsent is when they glean the essence of someone. Clairscent is when they have a clear smell. Clairgustant is when they have a clear taste. Clairtangent is when they have a clear touch. All mediums get their information in their own individual way. Mediums typically experience a combination of the Clairs.

CHAPTER 17

I Did Not Know

Now to let another dear friend in on this unbelievable discovery. I wanted to share what I was learning with anyone who might be interested in this information. So on a Wednesday evening during the following January, I took a friend of mine to see Robert Hansen in a group situation. We may or may not be read, but we would certainly see him in action and experience others being read, even if we were not. And I wanted my dear friend to experience this.

This time it turned out that I was one of the people that was going to be read by Robert though. He came over to me. He asked who Donald was. I said that is my father-in-law's name. He asked if my mother-in-law had crossed. I said, yes. He told me that she was conveying several things. One was the name "Ralph." Robert asked who that was to me. I said, "Ralph is my husband." He asked, "Who is the

Gemini?" My mother-in-law was showing him twins, he said. My nephew, on Ralph's side, is a Gemini. Then he said there is a living child with a severe case of cancer. I see holes in her head, holes in her skull and no eyes. I said my niece is legally blind after being treated very aggressively for cancer as an infant. He asked if it had been brain cancer. I said no, although yes, it had spread to the brain. He was so spot-on that my friend was amazed. I was intently listening to message after message for me. My heart felt like it was in my throat. I was shaking with nervousness. I had been read briefly by Josephine a few times now, but Robert's direct style had me at the edge of my seat.

He continued and said that my mother-in-law was there with others and that they were showing him a Lionel train set. He asked if we decorated our house at holiday time with a train set. I said, "No." He asked if my parents had decorated the home at holiday time with a train set when I was younger. I said, "No." He insisted that they were showing him a Lionel train set. He asked if I had ever gone on vacation with my mother-in-law and had taken an old fashioned steam engine train ride. I said that my husband and I had done this with our children, but I don't think my mother-in-law was with us at the time. He kept it up and up. I did not know what to say, but he would not quit. He said

I am seeing a man's hand holding a Lionel train car. He asked if I was sure that I did not have them in my house at all. I said that I did not, I was sure. He went on to ask me if my mother-in-law's name was Lucille. Yes, it was.

On the drive home, my friend was shocked at how accurate his information was. I was happy for her to see how the afterlife is so apparent/at least possible. How else would he have known all of this information? I told her that the only thing I found uncomfortable was his insistence on the train. Maybe that information was for someone else, but I wish he would have backed off sooner than he did, once he saw he was not ringing any bells for me.

The next Sunday, I went to visit my parents. I was letting them know about the fascinating group and individual reading that I shared with my friend that week. I explained the numerous precise hits, down to the specific names of Donald, Ralph, and Lucille. I also spoke about the miss. Robert kept bringing up a Lionel train. He was so persistent, even though the message was not for me. My father quickly said, "What?" in a lively manner. I repeated the train story. I said that he was being shown a man's hand holding a Lionel train. My father was stunned. He then proceeded to tell my mother and me a story about his week. He said, "Earlier this week, I was cleaning out the basement, and I found the box of Steven's old Lionel train set." Steven is my brother. That box had not been touched in decades. My father said he opened the box and held a train car in his hand, trying to figure out whether to keep the box of train cars or to throw it away.

I was now stunned also! My father asked me, "What are you telling me? That, someone, was downstairs in the basement watching me?" I did not know how to respond. I said, "Dad, I don't know what I am telling you." I was dumbfounded. So Robert going on and on about this train thing was not a miss after all? I was amazed. There was no way for me to have even known about this train box in the basement discovery.

We sat there in silence. Not even understanding the extent of it all...

If we survive death, then why are we on Earth to begin with?

CHAPTER 18

Like-Minded People

I had transitioned in that year or so from not thinking about the afterlife to believing it was real. Now I wanted to learn more about it. For the next three years, I spent thousands of dollars. I read any books that I was able to get my hands on and that I was able to get through. I went to metaphysical classes and group readings. I went to many mediums to see the differences and different styles. I learned that "Ralph" must be an easy name for the various mediums to hear. At least four mediums asked me, "Who is Ralph?" I learned that my mother-in-law was determined at every opportunity to help me understand what was occurring. She was walking this left-side brain of mine with little or no premonition ability down a path to understand and to accept that which I could not see, touch, or hear.

I was following the websites of the mediums that I had seen. I would spend my free time reading and soaking up any information I could find. After a little research, I saw that Robert Hansen had been a member of an international non-profit whose founders were only about a half-hour drive from my house. The mission of the foundation is to scientifically prove that there is an afterlife. This kind of organization was right up my alley. Scientific proof would lend credibility to my thoughts. I began to research this organization.

It had been started in 2004 after a local couple's 15-year-old daughter, Bailey Ginsberg, passed in a car crash. Whereas her mother, Phran, had some metaphysical tendencies, her father, Bob, had absolutely none. He thought the possibility of an afterlife was absurd. However, after his young daughter died, the signs were coming full force. He was determined to figure out what was going on. So, he began to research and learn. In short order, Bob came across a medium, who channeled his daughter with such specificity that he simply could not deny the possibility of an afterlife. So he and his wife began this foundation to move the needle on the public's acceptance of the afterlife.

I was particularly attracted to Bob's story. His analytical, left-brain was dominant; however, he began learning things that opened his eyes to what he could not see. This journey was what was occurring for me also. Forever Family Foundation is an international organization, which started very locally to me. It hosts different events. One, in particular, is called Afterlife Discussion Groups. It is an informal gathering with a facilitator, where like-minded people would get together to discuss their thoughts about the afterlife. It is a safe space to share ideas and happenings. I marked the date of the upcoming one on my calendar.

I went to the Afterlife Discussion Group session. It was located in a meeting room in the basement of a local library. There were about a dozen people there. The facilitators were the founders. I was fortunate that they lived near me. I learned that Forever Family Foundation has these discussion groups located in various areas of the country, so it was a coincidence that the founders themselves facilitated the one closest to my home. Phran reminded me of my mother-in-law. She has similar features. She is petite with black hair and very pale skin.

The meeting was two hours, and everyone was openly speaking about their own experiences, signs from loved ones, their theories, and things of that nature. One woman had two near-death experiences. Another woman said that she once visited the other side in her dream escorted by her recently deceased boyfriend.

When they spoke, they both mentioned seeing a bright light and walking to it in sort of a tunnel. I had heard of that type of thing, but to listen to these two women speak about it in person was fascinating. They did not know one another. They were approaching their experiences from very different perspectives. Yet they were saying similar things.

I recalled that I had heard a guest speaker once, a young woman, who made it her life's work to study people during times of disaster. The September 11th attacks had inspired her to see if she could learn how people respond when they are under pressure. She wanted to understand how and why some people made split-second decisions that resulted in their surviving, while others made split-second decisions that resulted in their deaths. I recalled something about tunnel vision during times of intense disaster. She had written a book, and I knew that I had it at home. I searched for the book that evening and found it on my shelf.

Sure enough, she had interviewed dozens of people who had survived disasters. Her interviewees had survived September 11th, wars, earthquakes, tornadoes, transportation accidents, and things of that nature. She found commonalities in their experiences. One similarity, in particular, was that they all said that of their five senses, sight, hearing, taste, smell, and touch, when under extreme duress, four senses would diminish rapidly, and one of the five senses would surface as almost a super-sense. That one sense would become so in tune with the person's surroundings that they would rely on that sense solely. For some, it was the sense of hearing, but for most, it was their sense of sight. In particular, their peripheral vision would not be present. They would only see what was directly in their line of sight. But they would see what was directly in their line of sight with unbelievable clarity and sharpness. It was called tunnel vision. The area that would ordinarily be part of their peripheral vision would become dark, so the area directly in front of them would become very bright and more crystal clear than they would ordinarily be able to see.

Hmm, I wondered if when people were experiencing a near death experience, this stressful situation might cause this type of reaction. I began to read book after book of accounts of near death experiences. I learned that near death experiences offer some of the most compelling evidence for life after death. People who are clinically dead (no brain waves, no respiration, no heartbeat, no reflexes) have clear and lucid experiences that they are able to convey. Near death experiences cannot be explained by medical science. How is it possible for a person who has no brain function to exhibit clear thinking or to meet their deceased relatives or to have any experiences at all?

Even more fascinating is that there are hundreds of accounts of near death experiences, and most have similarities to one another. These people are from different countries, different religions, different backgrounds, and different age groups, yet the overwhelming majority say that they enter a place of bright light where their deceased loved ones meet them. They say that it is a beautiful place where they experience a feeling of love and peace that they cannot explain. The feeling is as if they know somehow that they are going back home. Most recall conversations that include their being informed that it is not their time and that they will be going back to their human form.

I am a practical person. Although I did not think that I would believe in the afterlife when my journey first began, I found it increasingly impossible to believe that the mediums that I went to could have the detailed information about my family and me in any way other than their being told by my deceased loved ones. I read book after book, article after article, and heard first-hand accounts at the Afterlife Discussion Group sessions about near death experiences. Although not everyone's near death experiences were identical, I was confronted with a staggering number of reports which were similar to one another. I found it impossible that all of these various authors had conspired in some way to write these books over spans of decades so that their accounts were similar. I found it equally impossible that the near death experiencers had colluded to all recount these same experiences. That meant that these people were catching a glimpse of what occurs when we die. Fascinating.

I began and continue to volunteer my time to the Forever Family Foundation in any way that they need me. I could see that the mission to discuss this life-changing information openly would help people live their lives more fully and would also help them during times of grief about a loved one's death. I also saw that there are others, like me, on a quest to understand it all. There were still so many questions that I had. If my deceased loved ones are still around, then where exactly are they? How involved are they in my life? What are they doing now? If we survive, then why are we on Earth to begin with? How does our life relate to their lives?

CHAPTER 19

New Year's Eve

I continued my quest to understand more by zoning in on the time during my first medium experience with Josephine. She said that when we meditated on particular items by placing them in the palms of the hands of our deceased loved ones in our mind's eye, they would show us our sign within two weeks. It had happened with the orange monarch butterfly and the quarter, but could that be replicated?

I decided to test it on an upcoming New Year's Eve. I knew that my husband's family would spend midnight with us, as we had done for years. However, my mother-in-law was now passed, so she was absent. Or was she? I decided to see if I might be able to communicate with my mother-in-law and ask her to convey signs to me at a particular time. I asked her repeatedly on the days before New Year's Eve to show me a sign that she was still hanging out with us. I asked her out loud in my car on my way to work, saying her name and my request. I asked her in my mind while I was falling asleep at night also. I asked her to show me that she was there.

Then the day finally arrived. On New Year's Eve, our family arrived. I dared not tell them about my plan to include my deceased mother-in-law. I was concerned that if it did not work, then our fledgling learnings about the afterlife would be dashed. So, we all chatted, watched the television and ate lots of delicious food. I silently waited for the sign, hopeful that it would come. I had no idea what in particular I was looking for, but I was optimistic that I would recognize it when it arrived.

We were watching a New Years' special on a national television channel, which I thought was on all evening. It turns out that at 11 pm, they break into the special for a half-hour of the local news. The woman reporter was Lucille Wang. Her name kept appearing on the television. It said Lucille over and over again. My husband's family remarked that this was a sign since we all immediately thought of my mother-in-law, whose name was Lucille. I also thought that maybe this was the sign, but I was not satisfied.

Then a commercial came on about a television show featuring an actress named Lucy Lu. Now, I was nervous.

These seemed to be definite signs. However, the more mind-blowing aspect to me was that I had asked for signs, and they were appearing. It's one thing to receive signs. That is wonderful and that was becoming more believable to me. However, it is an entirely different thing to be able to ask to receive signs at a specified time and to have them appear. My mother-in-law was showing me one more important piece of information. If you ask for specific things and if the other side can help, they absolutely will. This information opened a new world of possibilities.

I shared the information with my friend, Meredith. She tried it. She asked her aunt, who had died many years ago, to show her hearts. About a week after her request, Meredith received a solicitation letter from the American Heart Association. She opened it and confetti hearts fell out.

I shared the information with my skeptical sister. She decided to ask our grandmother for seahorses. She figured that there would be almost no possibility of seeing that obscure item, let alone in a short two-week time frame. That week, my sister's co-worker came in with her vacation photos. She had visited an aquarium while on her vacation. And yes, she had photographed the seahorse display.

CHAPTER 20

Confession

I was raised as a Roman Catholic with all of the traditions of that religion. I attended church regularly. I enjoyed the habit of it. I enjoyed taking the time from a busy week to sit in the congregation and to focus on prayers and private thoughts. In recent years, the scandal of priests abusing altar boys was turning me off to the church and their cover-ups. I still attended mass throughout the time that the scandals were breaking though, and I would insist my family of four attended with me.

Holy Monday is the Monday during the week before Easter. On that day, the confessionals would be available all day to accept confessions before the Holy Mass on Easter Sunday. I always took advantage of that event to sit with a priest, to confess my sins, and to be blessed. So, on Holy Monday, I rushed home from work to head to confession with my then 15-year-old daughter before taking her to her dance classes later that evening.

Confession typically takes 20 minutes or so, depending on the line. When it was one's turn, the actual confessing of your sins to the priest and his blessings would take only two or three minutes. Then one would head to the church pew to pray a bit before heading on with their day. During the actual confession, the priest was typically behind a darkened screen. I think this way, a person would be comfortable confessing their deepest darkest secrets. On occasion, they would have the opportunity for an open confession if a parishioner wanted. This meant you would be face to face with the priest in a private room inside the church.

One's First Confession preceded one's First Holy Communion when a child was eight years of age. I recall telling my two children when they were nervous and heading in to their First Confessions that they should convey to the priest that they were too young to have any sins. To provide an example, I let them know that I have had the same two sins for most of my life. I can be impatient and I can lose my temper too quickly. It doesn't happen often, but when I would lose my temper, I would get curt and snap at my family members. Nothing too hurtful or spiteful, but being abrupt with anyone in one's family isn't kind.

That particular Holy Monday, there happened to be the opportunity for an open confession, which I decided to take advantage of. After my daughter was finished with her confession and she was praying in the pews, I entered the private room. A young priest was seated there. I said my prayers in front of him and then proceeded to tell him my two ever repeating sins. The priest engaged in conversation. They don't typically do that. He asked me what type of activities I am involved in that may help to reduce my stress, so that I would not lose my patience. I told him that with working full time and having a young family, I don't have a lot of time for extracurricular activities. He kept pursuing. He asked again what I did in my free time. What hobbies do I have? Do I engage in sports?

I decided to let him in on my latest pastime, my pursuit of learning as much as I can about what happens after we die. He asked how I was attaining the knowledge. I told him that I was reading dozens of books, attending medium group sessions with dozens of mediums, attending dozens of psychic ability classes, scouring the internet for related content, speaking with dozens of people about their experiences, and things of that nature. He got visibly upset. He asked me, "You are not paying money to go to these mediums, and these classes, are you?" Yes, I was paying money to attend classes, to buy books on the subject and to frequent medium events. These things aren't free of charge. So, I replied, "Yes, I am."

He told me that my pastime was harmful to me. He said that when we die, our souls should be left alone to rest in peace. He told me that the mediums, book companies, and psychics are just out for my money. He placed his hand on my forehead to bless me. I was shocked and a bit scared. He was requesting that I promise him that I cease and desist my pursuit immediately. I countered slightly by saying that what I was finding is that there really is a life after we die and that our loved ones' souls are still very much involved with our lives on earth. I let him know that I was finding that our deceased loved ones enjoy helping us out. He was not comfortable with that thought. He said God is the only one that can help us. He was getting more upset. He was surprised that I had any comeback, instead of just adopting his perspective.

I understand that a priest is an authority figure. I respect priests, of course. I respected him, but I also knew that he was not accurate. There certainly are mediums, psychics, and book companies that are frauds or are in it for their monetary gain only, but most are not. Most are only asking that they are paid for their time, as in any other profession.

If there are 100 mediums and 99 are fraudulent, but one is not, well, what does that mean for all of us? It means that if the authentic one is vigorously in touch with our loved ones, then our loved ones are still around and active in our lives.

The priest would not give up on me. He asked me to substitute my pastime with stress-reducing activities. He suggested running. I told him that I am not a runner, and I don't plan to start that now in my life. He suggested jogging. No thank you on that front also. He suggested that I join a gym. I told him that I had been part of a gym for years. One day, I went there, and it had gone bankrupt. It was boarded up. Instead of being upset with the money I lost, I was surprised at my giddy exhilaration. I had an hour free to myself. My family was not expecting me. I could do whatever I wanted for an hour. It was at that moment that I decided that the gym life was not really for me. I explained that I enjoy my exercises outdoors. I walk and I play golf; however, I still am intent on discovering all that I can about what happens after we die.

He was still asking me vehemently to cease and desist with my current pastime. I suddenly remembered that my daughter was waiting for me in the church. I had to get to her dance class. I had to get going. I could think of no other way to get out of the confessional other than to lie. I said, ok, I will cease and desist. He was visibly relieved that he had persuaded me to cease and desist my discovery of the afterlife. He gave me my penance and an extra blessing, and let me go on with my day.

I said my prayers and drove my daughter to her dance class. When I was home that evening, I called my friend, Donna. I let her know what had happened. I thought that maybe the particular priest that I made my confession with was opposed to the discovery of the afterlife. I was hoping that other religious people would not think similarly. Donna is religious and she also is the friend that I had first spoken to about the afterlife. She was so sure about its existence. She informed me that our religion actually is opposed to this type of dialogue. It conflicts with the Church's Heaven and Hell, Rest in Peace, and one God rhetoric. I was surprised. I had no idea. I thought the church would be in sync with the rise from the dead aspect of this all. She said it is one thing for Jesus, the Son of God, to rise from the dead. The general population rising from the dead is quite a different thing. That's true. I had not thought of that.

So great, now I have three sins to confess, I can be impatient, I can lose my temper too quickly, and I lied to a priest. I learned that organized religion is not the same thing as spirituality. This taught me that religion and spirituality are quite different from one another. Spiritually is not beholden to or part of any one particular religion. It is part of all religions and it is part of no religions. I was beginning to understand how our deceased loved ones were still around us. I was curious about how close they were and how timely their presence was. I couldn't cease and desist. I was drawn to pursue as much knowledge as I could. This was too life-changing to leave to chance.

We must move ahead. It is our only option.

CHAPTER 21

Spirit Guides

I did not want to believe in Spirit Guides before I started all of this, but the more that I learned, the more I had to believe in them. The concept of Spirit Guides seemed really out of this world and crazy to me. However, after some research and a particular experience, I understood that we all do have Spirit Guides.

I might have believed in Guardian Angels because they seem sort of heavenly and nondescript in nature. Guardian Angels seem a bit more random in terms of who has them and who does not. They are likely someone that you knew while on earth, but who has died and is now looking after you. So one was lucky if they were fortunate enough to have a Guardian Angel. However, Spirit Guides aren't hit or miss. They aren't based on luck, good fortune or having lost a loved one who would now look over you. From what

I had heard and read, anyone and everyone has Spirit Guides. That seemed more impossible to me.

However, the more I understood about the afterlife, the more I understood that we do all have Spirit Guides. So what does this mean? Who are our Spirit Guides? Spirit Guides can be people we knew while here on earth in a past lifetime. However, they are more likely souls who we have never met during our time on earth, but we know from the Other Side. Some Spirit Guides may guide us for our entire human lifetime. These lifelong Spirit Guides are with us for all of our time here, from birth until we cross back. Other Spirit Guides may guide us for certain and specific points in time during our human lifetime. For instance, it may be that a particular Spirit Guide's role is to help us when our children are young. They will guide us during that time, but not before or after that. We each also have our own individual Spirit Guides. They attend just to our soul, guiding us gently. They never judge us. They offer guidance constantly and consistently while we live our lives on earth. They will guide, but not force us because they also constantly and consistently respect our free will.

I had one occasion when I saw one of my Spirit Guides in a dream. The dream contained a crystal clear message. It was a decade ago, but I can envision it even today. The message was pointed, clear, concise, and powerful. I woke up immediately after the dream. Although it was the middle of the night, I got out of bed to find a paper and pen to write down the message. I wanted to make certain that I remembered it.

That evening, as I was falling asleep, my daughter came into my room. She seemed excited. Her girlfriend, Jennifer, had just received the good news that he was promoted to a higher level dance troupe. Diana was 16 years old. Diana and Jennifer had danced in the same troupe for about three years. They had become one another's best friends in their travel dance troupe. Having the same dance schedules, they traveled together, bunked together, and spent their free time during the dance competitions together.

Now that would all be changing. I was rife with emotions. I was happy for Jennifer. However, I was upset about their friendship and for my daughter. I was feeling a bit angry at the owner of the dance studio. Why would she promote Jennifer and not Diana? They were comparable dancers, although with differing dance disciplines. Diana was an unbelievable tap dancer. Jennifer was a wonderful modern style dancer. Maybe the owner wanted that modern style complement on the higher level team. But why break up their tight friendship?

I was concerned about conveying any of my mixed emotions to my daughter. So, while I was lying in bed, I quietly asked my daughter, "What do you feel about that?" She thought for a minute and then said, "I'm happy for Jennifer." I was happy that I did not convey that my emotions were mixed. I did not want Diana to have to process her feelings about my concerns, in addition to having to work through the feelings that she must be having.

I fell asleep, but I was upset. I was planning on reaching out to the owner the next day to ask if she would consider promoting Diana also. I was anticipating the conversation over and over in my head while falling asleep.

In the middle of that night, I had the dream. It was quick and yet conveyed a massive concept. There was a man in the dream. He looked to be about 35 years old with straight dark brown shoulder length hair. He was handsome with dark brown eyes and a narrow nose. He was wearing a brown fur type of sleeveless vest with tie clasps. He looked into my eyes quite forcefully. He said, "Drop it!" He said it in a very demanding manner. I looked directly into his eyes. I felt that he was from the place where my deceased mother-in-law also resided. It was as if the message was coming from both of them, although I only saw and heard him. It happened fast and I was a bit confused by what he meant. I said, "What?" He said again, "Drop it!"

I was still confused. I looked at this fellow with a question mark on my face. He then motioned for me to look downward. It is difficult for me to explain what he showed me. I was looking into the middle of a light brown vortex that was in the middle of a black-type of an infinite abyss. Years later, I saw a picture of a drawing called the "Whirlpool Galaxy." That drawing reminded me of what I was shown in my dream; however, the image in my dream was long and narrow, whereas the Whirlpool Galaxy looks more flat. The image in my dream was whirling at a very high speed, like lightning speed. So it was like I was looking down a whirling tunnel, or a whirlpool or the inside of a tornado.

Then, this good-looking fellow said to me, "You cannot recreate the living spirit." I immediately knew what he meant. He meant that life moves on and on. In every instant, things are changing. They may be changing in our life, the life of a loved one, or the life of a stranger. However, with each second that passes, things change. We cannot go backward and recreate the circumstances of a year ago, or a day ago, or of even a moment ago. The accumulation of all of our lives forms one massive living spirit. This swirling spirit is so forceful. Nothing can stop or pause it. It will swirl ahead, no matter how much we want to go back and recreate something that used to be. We cannot. We will never be able to do that. We must move ahead. It is our only option.

At the moment that he showed me that vortex, I understood so much. This concept is also difficult for me to explain. Somehow I went from being confused about his forceful message to having an absolute and complete understanding in an instant. I was awakened immediately afterward. It was about 3 am. I ran into my closet to grab a pen and paper to write it down, so I would not forget. "Drop it. You cannot recreate the living spirit." I went back to sleep. When I woke up the following morning, I had no concern about my daughter and her dance troupe. I realized deep inside of me that we couldn't go backward. We would move forward under these new circumstances. It was all we could do. I was totally at peace with that. Although I had fallen asleep with a lot of anxiety about the dance troupe changes, I had no trepidation now.

This realization is a significant concept. It has helped me innumerable times in my life since that dream. I am now quite comfortable moving forward, even when experiencing difficult circumstances. I understand in my core that we cannot go backward. We tend to think about our existence, and we long to go back to have what we used to have or what we just had. However, we are all connected. Even though only one thing may have changed for us in a minute, millions of things have changed in that same minute for us, for our loved ones and for strangers. Too much has changed from even a moment ago. We are a living spirit. We, the people, all together, are a living spirit. And we cannot reverse our course. We cannot recreate the living spirit.

To receive such a powerful life-changing message, I realized that this handsome fellow who also seemed to have my mother-in-law's essence was someone from the Other Side. He was one of my Spirit Guides. I don't know if he's just mine. I don't know if he only was there to convey this message for me and now has no involvement in my existence anymore. I don't know if he has a name. I don't know if I'll ever see him again. I just know that he was not anyone that I know here on earth. I also know that he was working with my mother-in-law to get this poignant message to me in a forceful way that would change my entire view of life-changing events. I felt tiny, humble, and supremely important all at once.

You cannot recreate the living spirit.

CHAPTER 22

Frogs

I was cleaning out the tank of our pet frogs. We had three frogs that we grew from mail-away tadpoles. The promotional material stated that they typically would not live more than a year. Ours were alive for eight years and counting. The promotional material said that in most cases, the females, who are the larger of this species, died upon shipment, so the smaller males would be the ones that survived the year. We had two males and one female. The female was about twice the size of the males. Cleaning their tank was disgusting. I cleaned it once a month with rubber gloves and a great deal of paraphernalia.

That particular evening after work, I was cleaning the tank, and Buddy, our female frog, escaped. She hopped onto the kitchen floor. I screamed very loudly for my son to help. "Joseph, Joseph, please come to the kitchen to help me. Buddy escaped!!" We were able to catch her and place her in the temporary tank with the two males, so I was able to clean their main tank. Ugh, gross. What we do for our children.

The following evening, I was attending a small group reading in Josephine's office with a few friends. They were professional friends who I had told my afterlife stories to, and they wanted to attend a session. My friends and I were three of the group of ten guests all hoping for a reading. After a couple of readings, Josephine focused on me. She asked if I had an Uncle Tony on the other side. Yes, he had died last year. My Uncle Tony was married to my mother's sister. They lived a few blocks from us. We are a very close family, so we spent many everyday and special occasions with my aunt, my uncle and my cousins.

Josephine said that my Uncle Tony was showing her that I had some type of exotic pet. I said no, I don't have any exotic pets. I was thinking of a pet monkey or an exotic lizard of some type. She thought for a minute as if she was listening to something that we couldn't see or hear. She said he was showing her an exotic pet, like maybe turtles. I laughed. I had not thought of our frogs as exotic, but yes, I have frogs! Ok, not precisely turtles, but yes, very close. She asked if something happened recently where one fell out of the tank. Yes, it had happened just last night. She said, I am hearing that you were screaming, "Ralph,

Ralph," to come to help you with the frogs. Well, again, not exactly, but very close. I called "Joseph, Joseph." Joseph is my son. Ralph is my husband. Even though the words weren't exact, it was apparent these messages were for me. It's not like she was saying another name that meant nothing to me, like "Travis, Travis" or "Dorothy, Dorothy." She was saying my husband's name.

While it was interesting to me that she was on point for the most part, with slight discrepancies, the more significant point is that our loved ones are actively involved in our lives on a very current basis. My Uncle Tony was there with me in my house just yesterday when our frog jumped out of the tank. I was past the point of wondering if our loved ones were communicating with these mediums. After witnessing dozens of different mediums conveying hundreds of messages to hundreds of people, I could see that our loved ones were communicating with us through these mediums.

I noticed that the messages of most of our deceased loved ones seemed similar no matter who the loved one was and no matter who the medium was. Our loved ones seem to convey five basic messages. They provide evidential messages to show us that it was indeed them. They convey that they had survived death. They convey that they are fine, free of any earthly disabilities that they may have been encumbered with during their lifetime or near the end of their life here. They convey that they are part of our current life. And they convey that they love us.

Sometimes there would be a message asking the sitter to do something in particular, like visiting a doctor or to be more careful while driving. Sometimes there would be a message asking for forgiveness for how they behaved toward the sitter while they were here. However the basic five messages, accompanied by irrefutable personal detail, were consistent. Their messages are simple, yet so powerful. "It is me. I am still in your life. I love you." They provide specific and undeniable evidential information to prove to us that it is them speaking through the medium and that they are still most definitely in our current daily lives, in case we are resistant to the afterlife concepts. Then, once we are willing to believe that they are communicating with us, they convey simply and powerfully that they love us.

I was also comforted to learn that our beloved pets are there for us on the other side. Animals and pets have their own type of energy level, while here and while on the other side. I have heard and read that animals don't reincarnate as people or vice versa. However, I noticed during the many readings that I attended that our deceased pets can convey their essence to a medium to communicate a loving message to their owner. Our precious and beloved pets are pure unconditional and consistent love. They help us to endure this earthly life with its various challenges. My pet dog's soul actually visited me during my dream once to show me part of her true inner nature. Our family always remarks how polite our little black and white Havanese is. However, we also notice that when we take Domino for a walk, she is quite insistent on the direction that she wants us to walk. She will use all of her ten pound body to pull and pull us in a certain direction. Sometimes, she prevails and sometimes we pull her the way we are planning to walk. One evening, I had a dream that she was pregnant. Her belly opened and my little Domino gave birth to a little flat animal. It looked like a piece of paper. The little flat animal rolled over twice and became a tiny billy goat. It was the exact same coloring as our Domino. Black and white in the same places. The only difference was that Domino has a lot of hair and the baby billy goat in my dream had no hair. And Domino was slightly larger than the billy goat. I woke up immediately. I realized that Domino was showing me that she is quite stubborn like a billy goat! Our amazing pets can communicate with us in a way that we can relate to.

With each thing I learned, I wanted to learn more. I wanted to understand how this is all working. I proceeded to read dozens of books and articles about how mediums work and about afterlife concepts.

Our loved ones convey that they are part of our current life. And they convey that they love us.

CHAPTER 23

Soul Growth

In my continued quest to learn, I learned that some mediums are sort of well, fraudulent. Although they may have some mediumistic tendencies, their psychic proficiency is minimal. They take whatever messages they can get and attempt to decipher it for the sitter. They embellish and try to read cues provided by a grieving and eager sitter. When they receive a message, it might be a fragment or not exactly for the right person.

There are, however, many mediums with strong abilities. Souls find mediums with greater levels of proficiency more easily. These mediums have to learn to turn the spirits on when they are looking to provide messages and off when they are not looking to convey messages. Otherwise it can inhibit the human lives of the mediums. This skill of tuning into messages when wanted and tuning out when not wanted may take years to develop for the medium. These proficient mediums make requests of the spirits, and the spirits respect their requests. The mediums may ask to only hear the communications at the time of readings, for instance. The souls comply. If the mediums ask for only good messages, with no messages containing words about illness or death, the souls also comply.

The souls are quite polite and respectful. They understand that we are all on our own individual growth path. They will not interfere with our free will. They will not help us if it interferes with our growth path. This is an important concept. Souls will allow us to live our earthly lives and to achieve our purpose here. There may be times when something that we as humans may be asking for, however it conflicts with our soul's purpose. At those times, the souls will refrain from providing us with guidance. They are too respectful of our soul, even though we as humans may not understand what our purpose is. The next time that you are pleading for their comfort and help, if you are not receiving what you are asking for, it may be because your growth path will be hampered if you were actually to obtain what you are asking for.

This is an important concept to understand as we move through this human life. It is not about our life on earth. It is bigger than that. We are each growing and evolving on this side and on the other side. On this side, we are more dependent. We connect with one another more intensely in positive and negative ways. On the other side, that doesn't occur. On the other side, we are all more individually evolving. Souls will not interfere with one another's growth path, even if a human is begging to be interfered with. So, when you think that you need or want something that you are not receiving, step back to think about it. It is likely that you cannot or will not receive what you are asking for because obtaining it will interfere with your greater growth or it may interfere with someone else's greater growth.

UGH, this is a difficult concept to accept. Our minds and bodies seem to know what we need. This concept is saying that we may not know what we need or want, at least for our soul. This seems almost impossible to believe or comprehend. Some people call it our ego getting in the way. The ego in this case is our human mind and body. It is all we know here on earth. It is what we rely on for everything. Yet, it is separate from our soul. We sort of know this deep down. However there is no real concrete validation of our soul, while our mind and body feels very real and reliable.

I explain it this way. Let's say that you live in a house and you walk out of your front door. You stand on your porch. It snowed last night. Your front yard is glistening with beautiful white snow. The trees and their branches have white snow coating them. Everything looks like a postcard. Your mailbox has a coat of powdery-white snow on top of it. It is early, so there are no footsteps anywhere in the snow. You stand on the porch for a moment enjoying the beauty of the early morning and the snow-covered landscape.

Now picture that far outside of your vision, there is a clear acrylic sphere encasing 100% of your surroundings, including the landscape as far as you can see, including you and your house. Imagine that you and everything that you know and everything that you are experiencing is actually inside a snow globe that you cannot see. Imagine that your deceased loved ones are right on the other side of that clear sphere. That is what is occurring. We think life is all about us and what we can see, hear, and experience. It is not about us here at all. It is about a life that is far bigger and far more different from our earthly lives. Our earthly lives are important, of course, however they are a slice or section of a larger picture.

Our loved ones are right there with us also. One medium explained it this way. He said that he was attending his daughter's dance class during a session when the parents were invited to attend. The children's dance session was followed by a pizza party. When the children were finished performing, the dance instructor let the parents know that they could come across the room from where they were seated in rows to enjoy the pizza across the room. This medium lagged behind the other parents to take a moment to soak up the scene unfolding in front of him. He saw the children who had just performed eagerly going to get their slices of pizza. He saw the parents, including his wife, headed to their children to provide accolades for a wonderful performance and to enjoy some pizza also. He just enjoyed the moment. Then a flood of souls said to him, "This is exactly how it is for us." They are right there with us. They are just soaking it all in. We are going about our daily routines, enjoying our families, eating our meals, going to work. We are involved in our lives and not realizing that they are right there. Our loved ones are right there watching our day unfold, just soaking it all in. They are enjoying our good times and comforting us as best as they can through our difficult times.

The souls are quite polite and respectful. They understand that we are all on our own individual growth path.

CHAPTER 24

Career Help from Heaven

My husband, Ralph, and I are both certified public accountants by training. Early on in our careers, we each transitioned to specific industries. I work in the healthcare industry, and my husband works in the financial industry. He became a bond trader around the time that our children were born. It is a rigorous and draining profession. It is fine when a person is younger and has more energy. However, people leave that particular profession as they age, since they often begin to burn out. After ten years in that profession, my husband began mentioning to me that he would like to find a slower-paced job; however, there were simply none that made any sense for him. He continued to labor in the high-pressured position of bond trader, keeping up his time-consuming and fast pace.

A year after his mother died, a professional friend of Ralph's asked him to meet for a drink on a day in the upcoming weeks. The weekday evening that his friend arranged happened to be on Ralph's birthday in November; however, his friend was not aware of that. They both worked in Manhattan, so they met at a restaurant there. Ralph's friend, Alan, had an opening in his department in the investment division of a large insurance company. Alan knew that Ralph knew a lot of people in the financial industry. Alan wanted to brainstorm a bit with Ralph to see if between the both of them they might be able to think of someone that might fit the position. Alan and Ralph knew many of the same people, so they spoke about colleague after colleague. Nobody was a perfect fit, but they agreed that some possible people might qualify, and that they might be interested. It would never have crossed Alan's mind that Ralph might be interested because Ralph was earning a lot more money in his high-powered bond trading position than this new opportunity could offer.

During the upcoming weekend, Ralph began to think more about their conversation. He started telling me about their meeting and the opening at the insurance company. Ralph said something that caught my attention. He said if it were a higher paying job, he might consider it for himself. I questioned him as to why. He listed several reasons why this position might be a good move for himself. It would be a significant reduction in his stress level. He would not have as many work-related dinners to attend. It was a secure company, so he could finish out his career at this one company if it worked out. He already had a couple of friends there. The commute was a nice walkable mile from the main public transportation hub, so that brisk morning walk would be good exercise for him. The only downside was the money reduction.

I understand that reducing one's income is very stressful; however, we live below our means, so I was not too worried about that. Ralph said that he wanted to crunch some numbers to see how difficult it would be for us. It then dawned on me; this meeting occurred on his birthday. With my newly discovered afterlife involvement, I realized that this meeting was not coincidentally on his birthday. It was a birthday gift from his mother! Although she had died the year prior, she did not want to miss his birthday. I was so excited. I let him know, no need to crunch numbers. Our finances would work out. This was a gift with too many benefits. It had to be from his mother. My excitement about this possibility was just what Ralph needed to pursue this a bit more for himself. Ralph decided to speak with Alan more about the opportunity and to convey his interest.

Alan was quite surprised. He said, of course, Ralph would be a great fit; however, he was overqualified. Alan said that the pace was much slower than what Ralph was used to and that it would not satisfy Ralph. Ralph continued to convey his interest and asked to please be considered. Alan invited Ralph in for interviews with several executives. Over the upcoming months, Ralph interviewed with many people at this insurance company. He had to assure each interviewer that he was serious about slowing his pace, leaving bond trading, and yes, he would take a reduction in salary.

The insurance executives hesitated. They wanted to give him a chance, but they were concerned about this step for him. Ralph also hesitated several times during the interview process. He was concerned about this step himself. I kept encouraging him. "You have to take this opportunity if offered. It is a birthday gift from your mother. She must want you to slow down a bit. Don't worry about the finances. I am working and earning an income also. We'll be fine." After a grueling two months and two weeks of interviews and negotiating, they finally made him an offer that he accepted. Oh yes, and it was made to him on his mother's birthday in February! I was so excited to be getting the hang of this all! Our loved ones can and will help us with specific important things in life if and when they can!

We are all intricately connected. The details and chain of events that lead up to an occurrence, any occurrence can be quite elaborate.

CHAPTER 25

The Fourth Medium

We hosted Thanksgiving Dinner after my mother-in-law passed, as we have done for many years. We invited my family and my husband's family to our home for a wonderful feast. We shared stories and chatted for hours. This particular year, my sister-in-law, Laura, wanted to share a story with us. She knew that I was speaking openly about the afterlife and about the signs that our loved ones are capable of sending. She had an experience that she thought was interesting.

After her mother died, Laura began receiving telephone calls from a man who lived further east in our county. The name "Corseone" would show up on Laura's answering machine. When she picked up the phone, this man would apologize because he had called the wrong number yet again. The phone calls happened on most holidays and even once on my sister-in-law's birthday. After a couple of times, Laura began to speak with the man to understand what was occurring. He was an older man. He was trying to reach his sister, who lived out of state. Laura's telephone number was the same as his sister's, but Laura's was in the same area code as Mr. Corseone's telephone number, while his sister had an out-of-state area code. When he would forget to dial the area code, it would ring Laura's phone. He was calling to wish his sister Merry Christmas, Happy Easter, Happy Thanksgiving, and Happy New Year. That explained the holiday connection. The two unexplained aspects were: why did this only start to occur after my mother-in-law passed and why was there the random call from Mr. Corseone to his sister on Laura's birthday in early July. However, my sister-in-law was satisfied to hear from him every once in a while on holidays. She felt that somehow her mother was reaching out through these calls to wish her Happy Holidays also. I agreed.

I had purchased four tickets for a local show with an internationally recognized medium for a few weeks after Thanksgiving Day that particular year. I had purchased the tickets when they first went on sale in April of that year. I had purchased them for my husband, my teenage daughter, my teenage son, and me. The venue held 3,000 people. My daughter decided that she did not want to go. We invited

Laura since she had just shared with us that she was open to the afterlife concept. We certainly did not expect to be read. The venue was large. However, just to be around that energy is reaffirming.

We arrived at the event early to get settled in our seats. Every seat was occupied. It was a theater in the round and the stage was in the center. The place was bustling with energy, as John Edward walked out. He is world-renowned. He has authored several books and he was one of the first mediums to have a national television show. He also travels internationally sharing his mediumistic gift with people in many countries. To be able to see him in person was exciting for everyone. He began by explaining how he receives and conveys the messages, as most mediums do. They all seem to receive their information a bit differently from one another, so the overall introduction as to what we might expect was helpful. John Edward began reading after reading. His readings and precision were amazing. He was on point with his information. He was very specific and his messages were full of personal detail. In a room of 3,000 people, he was able to pinpoint who the message was for or at least within a couple of seats of that person. It was very impressive.

About halfway through the show, he turned to our large section of the audience. He pointed to several rows in front of us. He asked a woman to stand who was two rows in front of us. He wondered if the word "Barberry" meant anything to her. The woman was so excited that she jumped up and tried to get the message to fit for her. But it did not. She had no connection to the word "Barberry."

John then made a 180-degree turn and pointed to a section and a few rows of people across the circular room from us. He asked if "Barberry" meant anything to anyone. A woman and her thirty-something-year-old daughter stood up. The woman lived on Barberry St. He then turned back around to the woman that was still standing two rows in front of us. John asked if she knew the woman or her daughter seated across the arena. No. He said there is some connection here, and we're going to figure out what it is.

He turned back to the woman and her daughter across the theater from us. He asked where Barberry St was. They said in Hicksville. He turned to the woman in front of us and asked if she lived in Hicksville. No, she lived in Massapequa. He wondered where they both worked. No connection there either.

John turned back around to the woman and her daughter seated directly opposite the arena from us. He explained that he felt a pull between our section and the section directly across the room from us. He said that he would ask the souls to convey some additional detail, so that he would be able to decipher the connection. The souls came through. He said that he had a young man coming through who died in a bar brawl. He had been shot and was proclaiming his love for the two women. The younger woman began to sob. Her mother told the story. Her daughter had been engaged a few years prior. Her fiancé tried to break up a fight in a bar between two other people. Her fiancé was shot and killed during the brawl. Her fiancé was the one coming through. The fiancé acknowledged that the young woman, his former fiancée, had met another fellow and that she was now married to someone else. The deceased fiancé said that her husband was a good man and that he was happy that her husband was treating her so well. Then, John Edward turned to the woman in front of us. She was still standing. He asked if she had any connection to that story. She did not. Even though the women from Hicksville were getting a reading, John was intent on figuring out the connection between them and the woman in our section. That is where his message initially occurred, so he persisted.

John explained that when the women from Hicksville on the other side of the arena were telling the story, he was feeling a pull from behind him. He knew there was a connection to someone on this side of the room. He said that he would continue until he determined what the link was. He turned back to the woman and daughter across the arena. He said that the deceased fiancé was coming through with the name "John." They confirmed that his name was John. They said that his name was John Corseone.

My sister-in-law turned to me. She said, "Corseone is the name of the fellow calling me with the wrong number!" I immediately sprang up and actively motioned for Laura to stand. I knew the message was not for the woman two rows in front of us. It was for Laura! John Edward turned around seeing our commotion, and the helper with the microphone took it from the lady two rows in front of us and gave it to us.

He asked what our connection was to this story. Laura shyly mentioned the wrong number calls from a fellow named Corseone. There seemed to be no connection between the elderly Mr. Corseone making the errant phone calls, and this murdered fiancé, but John Edward was certain the messages were for us. He spent about ten minutes with us. He mentioned four people and four people only. My niece, my nephew, my daughter, and my son. My mother-in-law's four and only four grandchildren.

She said that she passed while we were having a birthday cake for someone. Yes, we were celebrating my son's birthday. After dinner and before the cake, my husband, his father, and his sister left to go to the Hospice

Center of the Hospital, where my mother-in-law had been for weeks. She died then with just the three of them at her side.

She said that she shared a birthday month with someone. Yes, she and my daughter were both February babies. She said that she was watching over the Gemini. My nephew is a Gemini.

She finished her messages by gushing about my niece. Melissa had been born with cancer. She was diagnosed at 13 months old. The cancer had metastasized. She miraculously lived through severe treatments. She was legally blind, with many glands removed, so she was always special. She had special needs, but she was just special. If you've had anyone special in your life, you may understand. She was a perpetual young child. She was full of love and acceptance, more so than any of the rest of our family. She was exuberant and beautiful. Her whole life was us. She loved us unconditionally, and we loved her in the same way. We were told that she had only a 15% chance of surviving to the age of five.

She defied those averages. She had graduated from her special high school after my mother-in-law died and before the John Edward show. He conveyed that my mother-in-law was saying that her accomplishments were nothing short of a miracle. My sister-in-law was humble and said that she was not certain that this message was about Melissa because it was not exactly a miracle. I was positive it was. Melissa's accomplishments were a miracle. My mother-in-law was proud and gushing. John Edward was conveying that congratulatory message.

Right after he acknowledged my mother-in-law's four grandchildren and before he closed with us, he added a quick ending note. He said, "Have fun in Florida. Are any of you going to Florida?" Yes, my husband was leaving the following day for a business trip to Florida!

John moved on to another reading. We sat there, dumbfounded. I had been confident about my afterlife knowledge, but I realized that what I knew was the tip of an iceberg. The number of intricate details that had to play out just perfectly for us to experience what we had just experienced at that show was unbelievable. Mr. Corseone's sister had to have the same telephone number as Laura, except for the area code. Mr. Corseone had to make errant calls by leaving off the area code for his out-of-state sister. Laura had to start a conversation to hear from him how he pronounced his name. Laura had to share the story with me on Thanksgiving a couple of weeks prior. If she had tried to convey it to me at the time at the show, I don't know if I would have been sure enough to stand up knowing it was my mother-in-law. John Edward had to be performing in our area. I had to purchase tickets to the event. The event was sold out, so I had purchased these tickets eight months in advance of the show. My daughter had to back out of attending, so we could offer the extra ticket to Laura.

The woman and her daughter from Hicksville, who we have no connection to, had to be there at the John Edward show. The deceased fiancé with the same last name, Corseone, had to come through. The medium had to be certain that he felt a pull from clear across the room of 3,000 people when he was speaking with the woman and her daughter. The synchronicities were overwhelming. I learned another significant concept. We are all intricately connected. The details and chain of events that lead up to an occurrence, any occurrence, can be quite elaborate. They may be things that we see and understand, however they also may be things that we don't see or understand. I also learned that some lessons and signs take time to unfold. We hope for things to occur in a matter of days, but what we had just experienced at this show took months and even years of errant telephone calls to play out.

Oh, and yes, the errant telephone calls never occurred again after the show.

The souls will be empathetic, however they will not interfere with the growth of another soul.

CHAPTER 26

Interconnectivity of Souls

I learned during the show that all of our connections are vast, and we cannot know them. I continued to read dozens of books to understand more about how the universe works. I wanted to understand our connections to other people and other souls. I realized that life is not just about our separate family units. I learned that the design of things that occur in our lives spans time. Some plans may span months. Some plans may span decades. This is a significant concept.

Let me provide an example of what I mean. Let us say an adult son is mysteriously murdered. Let us say that the police continue to investigate; however, they have no leads. After an amount of time, the police declare that this crime is unsolved. His distraught parents and family continue doing all that they can to learn anything about this crime.

They cannot give up the hope of finding the murderer. They launch local and widespread media campaigns. However the crime remains unsolved. Let us say his distraught parents pursue psychics and mediums for years. They are desperate for some shred of information to help lead them to the killer. They are haunted by the unknown circumstances of their son's death. However, no medium or psychic can come through with the murderer, which would otherwise allow the crime to be solved and closed. This seems torturous to the parents. Why would this most terrible of circumstances be allowed to occur? If their son still exists on the other side, can't he help? Can't he see the pleading and begging his family is doing? Can't he provide a clue for his family to help solve this crime? In addition, they have other deceased family members. And everyone has Spirit Guides. Why is no soul helping to solve this case?

The answer is that if the souls can help us, they will, however they will not interfere with any soul's growth path. So, unfortunately, in this case, solving this case at this juncture would likely inhibit or maybe even derail someone's growth path.

Maybe, just maybe, the crime will be solved at a future date by a young detective. Perhaps that is part of the design. Solving this cold case may be a crucial element of the young detective's growth path. If the medium came up with the name earlier, then the young detective's growth path would have been intercepted. The souls will not do that. They will not interfere with someone's growth path.

Another alternative as to why the medium would not be able to glean the name of the murderer to help solve the murder is that maybe one or both of the murdered son's parents' growth paths include an amount of growth due to living without the closure of knowing their son's murderer. As much as the parents want to know, the souls will not interfere with or short circuit either of their growth paths. It is not about here; it is about the other side. The souls will be empathetic to the pain of the parents; however, they recognize that they need to experience this pain to grow. The souls will not interfere with the growth of another soul.

UGH, this is a difficult concept to accept. We feel with all our bodies and minds that life is all about what we are experiencing here on earth. It is not about here though; it is about the other side. Our time here is a tiny fraction of our life on the other side.

This is how I explain this concept. Let us say you have a five-year-old child. He wants a candy bar. However, it is not something that you are going to allow him to eat at that early time of the morning, let's say. He begins to meltdown. He is screaming and crying. He desperately begs you for the candy bar. This goes on for over a half-hour. You can see that he desperately and sincerely wants that candy bar. You feel empathy for his desperate state; however, you have a greater knowledge about how that candy bar factors into his life. You have a perspective that he simply cannot have. You know that the candy bar means nothing. He will have it later that day. After that day, there will be so many more days for him to enjoy candy bars and so much more. He will go to school. He will grow up. He will get a job and contribute to society. He will fall in and out of love. He will lose loved ones during his lifetime. There are big life things that will occur. The candy bar means nothing. You recognize that. He does not. You console as best you can, but he has to move on.

That is how our deceased loved ones look and feel about us as we desperately beg for things to occur. That is how they view our deep grief about their crossing. They are empathetic for our troubled state; however, they have a greater knowledge about how this particular loss factors into the greater aspects of our life and growth path. I do not want to minimize anyone's feelings. Feelings are real, deep, and sincere. However, they are all part of our growth path, both the positive and the negative emotions. We are meant to work through many of them on our own with nobody else's help. Living this human existence provides an isolation from our greater collective and connected consciousness. We sort of think it may be there, however we are also protected from it. We forget who we are and where we came from, as we work through our human challenges.

Sometimes our human feelings can detract from our soul's purpose. I have an interesting example of this. I had the honor of being a volunteer at a medium event a few years ago. I ran around the room with the microphone and tissues to hand to the guests as the nationally-renowned medium, Laura Lynne Jackson, was doing her readings. Coincidentally, or likely not, every soul that came through was a child of someone in the room, ranging from eight to 30 years of age when they passed. There were about two hundred guests. Many were hoping that their parent, sibling, aunt, cousin would come through with a reading for them, however only young and adult children of guests came through. There were about 15 readings. There were undeniable evidential validations. The guests were validated over and over again. There were tears and gasps of amazement throughout the evening.

I noticed something very interesting while I was doing my job that evening. At least four of these child souls said the same thing to their respective parents. 'It was not your responsibility to protect me. It was only your responsibility to love me unconditionally. And I could not have chosen anyone better to do that.'

I was surprised, so I mentioned that to Laura Lynne afterward. She was so busy using all of her energy and her focus to channel what she was hearing. She had not focused on the fact that all of the deceased loved ones that came through were children. Some were young children, but some were adult children. Although she had not recalled those four in particular who had stated that their parents were not responsible for protecting their children's souls, she said that it made sense based on her knowledge of the universe and how we all relate to one another.

I felt that I had experienced something unique. I enjoyed a different vantage point than the others in the room that evening. The guests eagerly wanted their readings, so they were each hoping for their deceased loved ones to deliver a message. I had this interesting bird's eye view that others did not have. The message that I heard is so powerful. Parents feel responsible for protecting our children. Family members feel responsible for protecting our family members. However, protection and love are two different feelings. Protection comes from a place of fear. Love does not. Maybe our only, or at least our primary, responsibility is to love our children and our family members unconditionally. Maybe, that is it. We are not here to protect them, only to love and guide.

This is a difficult concept to appreciate because order of birth and rank within a family is a basic societal tenet. Any parent would say they are responsible for their child's protection. It seemed to me that evening that this was not the case. That children select a parent to love them unconditionally. Or maybe certain children select certain parents to love them unconditionally as their primary responsibility.

Your purpose or mission is not something that we as humans would ordinarily consider to be an achievement. When you choose to act from a place of pure kindness, forgiveness, and love, you are moving toward completing your purpose.

CHAPTER 27

Soul Choices

As I continued to expand my knowledge about the metaphysical world, I learned that we choose a few things before our arrival on earth. We decide who our family will be, we decide how and when we will cross back, and we determine what our purpose here is. Our family is typically members of our soul group. We have more of a vested interest in the growth of members of our soul groups. We are born into families that promote that growth. We become friendly and intimate with people that support our growth.

How and when we cross back may be something along the lines of a long illness in our 70's, a quick passing in our 50's, or as a young child. We may choose to be part of a group of souls who select to cross as part of a common event to raise spiritual awareness, as in the case of

September 11th, 2001, or in the case of a war. The COVID 19 pandemic showed us how all humans are connected, even though we may not see the connection. We all saw how the virus effortlessly raced across the world. The brave souls that crossed during those horrible circumstances likely had a pact prior to their arrival on earth. It was an intricate pact. It involved each of them, as an individual, as well as their families, the healthcare heroes, the grocery store workers, the delivery men and women, the truck drivers, the politicians and all those who were quarantined in their homes.

It was a massive effort showing us that although we cannot see the connection, all humans are connected. It showed us the value of society and of personal intimate relationships. Simple loving gestures that we take for granted, like a mask-less smile or a hug, became weapons. The COVID pandemic blatantly forced everyone to rethink and to reconfigure our daily routines and to spend time with a small unit of family and friends. The learning lessons during the pandemic are endless. We all owe those that passed a debt of gratitude.

Accomplishing our purpose helps our growth path. It often helps the growth path of others also.

Your purpose or mission is not something that we as humans would ordinarily consider to be an achievement.

We may fulfill our mission when we spend extra time with a co-worker helping them with a problem that they are having. We may achieve our purpose by caring for an ill parent. We may fulfill our mission by taking the time to speak to a stranger, not knowing that they are experiencing such deep sorrow that our conversation is helping them tremendously. When you choose to act from a place of pure kindness, forgiveness, and love, you are moving toward completing your purpose.

Souls may provide strangers with the karmic opportunity that they owe them from a previous life. If someone helps a dying person to cross over, both individuals may reincarnate specifically to allow the person who had crossed, the opportunity to help the person who had helped them to cross over. A seemingly Good Samaritan, who appears to be a stranger, may actually be performing a deed for another who he has met in a past life. We are all connected. Our lives are not as random as we may think.

Souls have decided how and when they return/die; however, every once in a while, a soul will die earlier than he originally agreed to. The only time that you may not have had the opportunity to complete your purpose is if you die by suicide.

Suicide, when terminally ill, is viewed differently than suicide when not terminally ill with respect to completing one's purpose. Suicide when not terminally ill may cut short one's ability to achieve one's mission(s). Suicide, when terminally ill, does not. However, when someone takes their life early due to terminal illness, they may be preventing someone else or their loved ones from the experience of a growth opportunity. Caring for someone that is terminally ill helps the caretaker's soul to grow also. Having said this, prayer from those on earth and from souls on the other side will help a soul that died by suicide to elevate their level of light. Prayer and pure thoughts of our loved ones, whether here or on the other side, always helps to raise a soul's level of light.

CHAPTER 28

The Telephone Call Means Something

Please allow me to pause and re-state that I am left-brain oriented with little or no traditional psychic abilities. I am simply someone who is in awe by why we are all here. I read hundreds of books and articles. I frequented dozens and dozens of medium events, meditation events, readings, and classes to garner as much knowledge as I could. Once I understood more about the universe, I began to see times when I was being used by the universe to help someone else. I find these times in my life to be some of the most rewarding occurrences for me.

I worked as the Chief Executive and Chief Financial Officer for a large physician-owned practice in New York State. The group was owned by about 20 physicians of varying ages and backgrounds. I was the main non-physician executive for over 20 years. I loved it.

I was to attend a fundraising event with one of the physician partners on a particular winter evening. It was postponed due to a snowstorm and it was rescheduled for two weeks later. I was able to attend; however, the physician partner who had originally intended to attend was not able to make the new day and time, so a different physician partner attended. He was a young physician. He had worked with our group for about three years. I knew him, but not very well.

We attended the fundraiser together. It was held in a large corporate building. It was crowded, so although we mainly stayed together, we were often conversing in separate groups also. We left at the same time though. It was about nine o'clock in the evening when we left. We made work-related small talk as we exited the suite, as we waited for the elevator, as we exited the elevator, and as we walked through the large lobby.

We transitioned to a personal level when I asked how his family was. He has a beautiful wife and three beautiful young daughters. He said that his family was well; however, he was going through a very difficult time because his father in Florida was ill. Dr. Schnell was not certain if it was a life-threatening illness, but it appeared that it might be. His father had been deteriorating for the past six months. Dr. Schnell was so concerned that he would not be there when his father died. Dr. Schnell had hired wonderful nurses to care for his father. Dr. Schnell was flying back and forth from New York to Florida almost every other weekend. He repeated that he would have a difficult time if his father died without his being there.

I could see his deep and sincere angst over this. I had learned that the details of when we cross back are already determined by our souls. In other words, his father had decided before he even came to the earth whether or not Dr. Schnell would be at his side at the time of his crossing back. It had nothing to do with Dr. Schnell's flying back and forth. If his father had determined he wanted his son there, then it would occur during one of these trips to Florida. If his father had decided that he did not want his son there, then it would happen when Dr. Schnell was in New York. I could see that Dr. Schnell was torturing himself about something that had nothing to do with his comings and goings. So, I ventured to the topic.

I was nervous to broach this topic with someone that I did not know that well. I was concerned because we worked together. I was unsure how this would impact his respect for me as a business executive. However, I knew that I had information that would help him. I knew that I could cull through the volumes of information that I had learned and that I could zero in on specific items to help him in this particular set of circumstances. I mustered the courage to say, "I want to let you know something. I do not mean to intrude, but since you brought up what you are going through with your father, I want you to know that there is no need for you to pressure yourself about flying back and forth at precise times. Your father has already determined whether you will or will not be at his side when he dies." Dr. Schnell stood there looking at me like I had two heads.

I nervously and quickly spoke to fill the awkward silence. "The thing is this, Dr. Schnell, my mother-in-law showed me after she died that there is an afterlife. She led me down a path where I have learned a lot of things about souls, the afterlife, why we are here, and things of that nature. And I just want to let you know that before we are each born, we decide a few things. One of them is how we will return home or die. So your father's soul already has determined whether you will be with him or not." Dr. Schnell was staring at me, studying my face in silence.

I was not certain if he was ok with what I was saying, but he was not walking away or shutting it down, which has occurred when I raised the topic with others. So, I assumed that he was considering what I was saying. I remained silent for a minute to see how he wanted to respond. Being a physician, he is scientific and smart. He asked, "How did your mother-in-law show you this?" I let him know it was a long story; however, I conveyed a summary of the pom-pom story. I told him that my mother-in-law helped with a series of synchronicities that led me down a path. I told him that the long and short of it is that I spent years and several thousand dollars reading materials and attending sessions to garner every bit of knowledge and experience that I was able to gather. I told him that I had not been certain about whether or not there was an afterlife when I began the journey, but I am certain now. We live on.

We were standing there in the lobby of this major corporate building, about 20 minutes into our solemn and intense conversation when his phone rang. He answered it. It was his father's nurse asking him if it was ok to give his father some type of medication or another. She let Dr. Schnell know that his father had a good day and that he was stable. She said that she would see Dr. Schnell that upcoming weekend since he was planning on visiting. When he got off of the telephone and conveyed the very ordinary content of his call, I immediately got a chill. I could pick up on this synchronicity. It was no coincidence that I was letting him in on this great information at the exact time that he received this call. I realized that his father was going to be passing away in the upcoming day or so. His father and the universe wanted me to convey this information, and they wanted Dr. Schnell to be receptive to it.

We continued to speak after he hung up the phone. I conveyed a few more anecdotes that supported my points. I also let him know that once his father crosses, his father will send signs to Dr. Schnell to show him that he is still around. I had heard that in some instances, they are prevalent in the first three days after passing. Dr. Schnell listened skeptically. At the end of our conversation, he thanked me. He said, "I am so surprised that this is coming from you. You are a CPA, and you are my CEO! It is not like you smoke pot or anything." That was a peculiar thing to say, I know. However, this was a strange topic. He was trying to connect my practical business side with this spiritual side. I understood. I have also been trying to connect these two distinctly different sides of myself since I began following all of this.

CHAPTER 29

Thank You to Me

The afternoon following our late-night conversation after the fundraiser, my assistant entered my office. She said, "Dr. Schnell's father died. He'll be heading to Florida." I immediately felt honored and humbled to have played my part in this design. I was also elated because I had understood the synchronicity at the time it was occurring. I had not even known that I had a job to do; however, I took the chance to broach this taboo topic with Dr. Schnell, and I had done my job well.

I understood that the initial date of the fundraiser was meant to be postponed, I realized that the physician that was originally intended to attend not being able to make it was meant to play out as it had. I understood that Dr. Schnell was expected to participate. I realized that he was meant to open up to me about his father. I understood that I was meant to convey the aspects of what I had learned that would help him during this difficult time in his life. The design was working as planned, and I was a little part of that.

Late that evening, Dr. Schnell texted me from Florida. He thanked me for the conversation. He said he had not been there when his father died; however, he was comfortable with that. He said he would not have been comfortable not being there at the time of his father's death if we had not had the conversation. He then said something that I found poignant and so heartwarming. He said that he understands that his father would not have wanted Dr. Schnell there when he crossed because his father would not have been comfortable with his son seeing him at that moment of physical weakness.

That was heartwarming to me. It meant that Dr. Schnell had not only listened to my stories, but he understood and accepted the part about our choice as to whether we want our loved ones there at the time of our crossing. Dr. Schnell had internalized that his father's crossing was not about how Dr. Schnell would have wanted it to transpire; it was instead about how his father wanted his own crossing to transpire. I felt so happy for him. I was so happy for me. The universe had used me in this wonderful way.

Over the next several days, Dr. Schnell continued to text me from Florida to tell me about a variety of signs that his father was sending. His father had a favorite made-for-television movie that had not been on for decades. Dr. Schnell could not sleep one evening. He turned on the television and, lo and behold, that old movie was on. He turned on the car radio while driving, and the host's name was the same very unique name as his father's. He found sign after sign. He attributed being able to pick up on these signs to our conversation. I was honored. I was happy for him.

He even said that he knows why his father chose to die on the specific day that he died. In the Jewish faith, the family mourns for a week. During that week, there would be no travel or anything of that nature. His father died one week and one day before Dr. Schnell had a family trip planned to Florida. His daughters had off from school the week of their planned trip, and Dr. Schnell's family was able to go since it was one day after the week of mourning.

At the New York-based service, which I attended, Dr. Schnell gave me a huge and sincere hug. He was appreciative of our timely conversation. All I did was convey a fraction of what I had learned that made sense in his particular circumstances. However, that conversation opened his eyes just enough so that his father, his loved ones, and Dr. Schnell himself could take care of validating the content of the conversation over the series of ensuing events.

I learned that every single human is here with something that their soul has to learn. It is true for you. It is true for me. It is true for everyone. There is no exception.

CHAPTER 30

Soul Groups

I read more and went to more classes to hear what various metaphysical people were saying about what they learned or knew. I was putting together tidbits of information that resonated with me. I discounted what did not make sense to me and what did not resonate with me. I was being used by the universe and I felt great about doing my part, so I wanted to understand more. Maybe I could help others.

I learned that we travel and grow with soul groups throughout our human and spiritual life. The inner soul groups are typically between three and 15 souls on a more intimate level. These inner soul groups are part of larger souls groups that we also travel and grow with. The larger souls groups have 100 - 200 souls. I did not want to have to believe in reincarnation; however, once I began delving into how the universe works for souls, I had no choice but to accept that reincarnation exists. I learned that most souls don't reincarnate readily. It can be 50 or more years after they die for a soul to reincarnate. Although time is something we only experience here on earth. Those 50 years are not anything of consequence on the other side.

Time is a human concept and measurement. It does not have a correlate concept on the other side. A moment and infinity are the same thing on the other side. We cannot possibly relate to this because time is essential to our human experience. Although we do experience a glimpse of how time can be perceived differently based on circumstances. This is an example and it has to do with Einstein's theory of relativity. In other words, we can only experience something when we are able to compare it to something that we can relate it to. We often hear people say that time seems to go faster as we age. Time flies. Where did this year go? I cannot believe that is has been a year since such and such. In reality, time *is* actually going faster for us as we age. Although a measurement of time, let us say a year, is always a year, 365 days, no matter when in our lives we experience it, that same year has a less significant correlation to what we can relate it to. For instance, a year when we are ten years of age is ten percent of our life, but a year when we are 50 years of age is only two percent of our life. That lesser percentage makes the year's passing seem faster to us because it is a lesser percentage of what we can relate it to. It is almost as if a measurement of time is less consequential as we age. On the other side, time is of no consequence.

I also learned that we all have a vested interest in the evolution of all other beings. The growth of our family, our neighbors, our co-workers, and strangers are important for our growth also. We are all connected. When one grows, we all grow. When one refuses to grow, we are all stalled. The reasons that we do not feel the repercussions too much are because we are diluted by the sheer quantity of souls in the universe and because as humans we are all absorbed in ourselves, our families, and our friends. We are distracted from our soul's importance, purpose and connection with all others because our daily lives typically take all of our human energy. Understanding our place in the universe is something we all can feel to some extent, but dealing with our human challenges and enjoying our human pleasures takes most of our energy.

I learned that every single human is here with something that their soul has to learn. In other words, no matter how fortunate someone seems to be, that person is struggling with a lesson or a demon that they are trying to conquer. You can see by just reading the news, that no matter the business success level, the family wealth, or the amount of fame that someone achieves, everyone has a struggle. We are all here to conquer our selfishness, lack of compassion, addictions, depression, insecurities, anger management, or anxieties. Some humans cannot help themselves from harming others. Some cannot help themselves from harming themselves.

Overcoming and conquering our demons or lessons is many times more difficult than just succumbing to the demons. Breaking that cycle and growing is what we are all trying to do. It is true for you. It is true for me. It is true for everyone in your family. It is true for your neighbors. It is true for your friends. It is true for everyone you meet. It is true for everyone who is famous. It is true for everyone. There is no exception. Unfortunately, it is not easy, however every step that we take toward that growth path, small or large, is a definite, concrete step forward. Moving forward is what we all do every day.

I learned that it is easier to grow when we are in our human form than when we are on the other side. This is because the other side has only positive aspects, while the earth has many negative aspects. Pain and suffering is a human experience. There is no pain or suffering on the other side. The souls on the other side, grow through meditation, prayers, education, and positive experiences.

While on this side, we also can improve through these mechanisms. However, in addition, we have negative experiences and burdens on this side. We have grief, pain, hurt, and sorrow on this side. We do not have that on the other side.

On earth, we recall the mistakes we make with clarity. We don't seem to remember our acts of kindness with the same precision. However, as a soul, it is inverted. We recall the kindness that others bestow on us with clarity. Seemingly small acts of kindness bestowed by any soul on earth or on the other side often make a significant impact on a soul, and the souls will remember. Acts of kindness are like deposits in a bank account.

Since growth occurs more rapidly when we are encouraged to suffer or encouraged to forgive, our souls come to earth to fast track our growth. Before our arrival to earth, there are intricate agreements that we make with other souls. The agreements are sometimes referred to as soul contracts.

An example might be that someone within our soul group agrees with us to help us grow at a more rapid pace. They may agree because we are lagging behind the rest of our soul group in terms of growth. If we are lagging in terms of growth, this would be slowing the growth of our entire inner and larger soul group. We may agree to come to earth to speed up our growth, so that we are able to catch up to the rest of our soul group. This is an important concept.

For example, a soul may agree to come to earth as another soul's child. The child soul may decide to die of leukemia at six years of age. This horrible situation forces the parent soul to live much of their adult life in grief. The parent must process through the stages of death. They must live every day of their lives with the unimaginable grief of losing a child. If they can navigate through the terrible tragedy, their souls will grow. Their souls grow at quite a rapid pace, possibly catching up to the growth path of the child who crossed at an early age.

The more rapid growth helps the soul's inner soul group and it helps their larger soul group to grow also. When we learn and grow, we grow in our level of light. Advancing our level of light is the overall purpose of our soul. When we are being kind, forgiving and loving, we are aligned with that purpose. I believe that the master energy source that we all originated from is the collective light energy of all of our souls in their brightest and their purest level of light. So no matter what you may call the master energy, for example, 'God' or 'Supreme Being,' I believe that 'Being' is us. It is collectively all of us and all of the souls of the universe in their most pure and most illuminated form. We, all together are the Creator, the Source, the Judges, and the Being that we are growing to return home to. It is where we óriginally came from and what we all aspire to return to.

On earth, we recall the mistakes we make with clarity. We don't seem to remember our acts of kindness with the same precision. However, as a soul, it is inverted. We recall the kindness that others bestow on us with clarity.

CHAPTER 31

Let's Work Together Again

Paul was our commercial real estate broker whose services we had utilized at work for about a decade. We had many offices, so over the years, Paul and I had the opportunity to develop a friendly professional relationship. Even though my company had not rented or purchased any real estate for three years, we now found ourselves in the market for a building rental. I reached out to Paul, which provided us the opportunity to re-connect. Although I had not spoken to him for three years, we caught up on one another's professional and personal lives quickly.

We began office shopping together. After about three weeks, he discovered that his father was terminally ill. Paul confided in me that his father might have only a year to live. Paul told me that he and his father had never been close, but somehow Paul was the only one in the position to be able to care for his father during the upcoming year. This situation created a conflict for Paul. He did not want to care for his father, but he felt it was his duty as a son. His father owned a business also so that aspect would pose an additional hassle for Paul.

I immediately realized that our business' need to find real estate at this pivotal time in Paul's life had a more poignant purpose. I was close enough to Paul that I felt comfortable conveying my recent afterlife discoveries. I knew that Paul's father had chosen this path for his crossing to provide Paul and him the last chance to heal their relationship before he died. I knew that I had to convey to Paul the bigger picture because I could see that he was agitating over the various business aspects of dying. The business aspects are tying up loose ends, going to doctors' appointments, paying bills, figuring out bank accounts, and dealing with the various medical and life insurance items. Paul is an astute businessman. He was perfect for figuring out all of those details. His father knew that. This was all part of the design. I was so happy that I could see it and that I knew the part I was to play.

I tentatively broached the topic over the telephone. I wanted to discuss this intense topic in person, instead of over the telephone, however Paul had disclosed his state of turmoil to me over the telephone. I knew that was my opportunity to at least bring the topic up. I asked Paul if we could get together for a drink. He was curious why I had turned the conversation from his deep topic about his father to my bringing up getting together. He pressed me as to why. I told him that after my mother-in-law died, she led me down a path to show me that there is an afterlife. I told him that I wanted to convey some of what I had learned to him because it may help in the upcoming months as he cared for his father. Paul was silent. I waited because I could not determine over the telephone if he was receptive or dismissive. "Really?!" He said incredulously. "Please tell me now." He was receptive.

I continued stating that I prefer to meet in person. I could not imagine speaking about this topic on the telephone and not being able to see Paul's reaction. I wanted to see first-hand if he thought that I was crazy. I have my business persona to be mindful of. However, my desire to help won over my fear. Paul was pressing for more information, so I conveyed a summary of the pom-pom story. The pom-pom story had become my go-to story to start the topic with most people. Then I explained that I had become intent on figuring this all out, so I spent thousands of dollars and countless hours reading books and going to events and classes. I discounted what did not make sense to me and retained what resonated with me. So now, I understand things about the universe that I had not before.

I told him that his father's soul selected how he would depart before his father was even born. I said it appeared to me that his father wanted to heal their relationship before he crossed back. Now that I was in tune with this type of thing, I had seen this scenario several times. Estranged parents and children reconciled just in time to have someone cross back. I let Paul know that his father knew that Paul was the perfect person for him to trust to wind down his father's business.

Paul listened intently. I paused to give Paul the opportunity to say something. Anything. I was hopeful that he was not passing judgment on my business skills. He was not. Not at all. He was appreciative and fascinated. He asked a few questions. He said that he had never been certain how he felt about the metaphysical world, but that he also had not thought about it too often. He then said, "I appreciate this coming from you. I would never have expected you to be into this type of thing." I knew what he meant. I am a left-brain dominant business woman. I would never have expected me to be into this type of thing either. However, I wanted to understand as much as I was able to about this life of ours. And once I started to learn, it became more and more amazing. Then once I had accumulated the knowledge, I can see it helps people that I care about.

CHAPTER 32

Dimes

Paul called me a few days after our telephone conversation. He was out of breath with excitement. He was whispering as if he did not want anyone to hear. He said that he had to tell me something and that I was the only one he could tell it to because of our conversation the other day.

He had taken his father for ice cream after one of his father's doctor appointments. It was a sunny fall afternoon. They sat outside on two benches facing one another and eating their ice cream cones. Then Paul said that a miracle happened. Paul saw his deceased grandmother in the air above his father's head. She was standing behind his father! Now I was shocked. Really!? He went from not thinking about the afterlife to being able to see visions. That is unbelievable. I asked questions. Which grandmother? His father's mother. What did she say? Nothing. How long was she there? A minute or two. Did Paul try to speak with her? No. Did Paul tell his father? No. What did Paul think it meant? Paul concluded that she was preparing Paul for his father's crossing. Paul said before she left, she looked at the ground between both of the benches and indicated with a head nod for Paul to look there also. He saw a solitary dime. He was not certain if that is what she wanted him to see, but he leaned over, picked it up, and put it in his pocket.

That was the end of his story. I was shocked. I was so happy for Paul. Maybe he had psychic abilities, and he never felt the permission to tap into them. I do not know, but I was happy for him because he was viewing the upcoming caretaking time in a very different light because of our conversation. I was happy for myself because I had seen what was occurring as it was occurring. I understood the role that I was to play. I was satisfied with myself because I played my role and performed my job well.

Paul called me a few days after that. He was at the gym. When he went to his locker to change out of his gym clothes and back into his street clothes, he found two dimes in his shoe. It made no sense to him because he would have had to be walking around with these two dimes in his shoe without being aware of them. They were not clinking in his shoe or bothering him in any way. He said that would be impossible. He recalled that his deceased grandmother had pointed out the dime between his father and himself while they were eating their ice creams. He attributed these new found dimes to his grandmother placing them there. He was amazed. He placed the dimes in his pocket and headed home from the gym. A few days after that, he found a dime in the middle of the stairs in his house. He said it would have been impossible for him to miss it there all day as he went up and down the steps before it appeared out of nowhere. A few days after that, he found a dime right by his alarm clock before setting it one night for the next morning. It was not there when he shut his alarm and left for work that morning. It was there when he went to set his alarm in the evening. He lived alone, so there was no explanation other than some otherworldly energy placing these dimes in his path. He called me each time. We marveled each time.

I thought that he was kidding with me. I believed in all this, but this pattern seemed unbelievable. He went from hearing about the afterlife from me a month earlier to experiencing a vision, and now this pattern of obviously placed dimes. I might believe it more easily if it were pennies, although even that would be interesting to me. Finding this many dimes repetitively was surprising. I could not recall finding that many dimes in my lifetime. I could say I would find a dime every once in a while, but not that often. In the meantime, his father was deteriorating, as Paul visited doctor after doctor with his father.

We had an upcoming real estate meeting with the landlord and the principals that I worked for. At the meeting, Paul pulled me aside, reached into his pocket, and showed me the nine dimes he had found to date. Some were found one at a time. Some were found in a group of two. The dimes looked like any other dimes, of course. However, they meant something so special to him. He attributed them to me in some way. However, I knew it was his family hard at work to help him through his current set of challenging circumstances.

It was the following Saturday morning after our business meeting of earlier that week. I was running my errands, as I ordinarily do. While exiting Target, a store that I frequent, I looked down. In the middle of the black carpet was a shiny silver dime. My heart jumped. It is not surprising to find a dime on the floor in a store. However, I immediately knew that this was not an ordinary dime. It was the tenth of Paul's dimes. And it was left for me to find. I picked it up and placed it in my pocket. I knew his father must have passed or was passing imminently. Someone in the universe, maybe his father, maybe his grandmother, maybe my mother-in-law was thanking me for a job well done.

This dime was from someone that I could not see. It was from someone who was somehow able to have someone else drop this dime and not realize it. It was timed for me to find it. Or maybe the souls were able to move that dime from somewhere and place it in my path. I do not know the mechanics, but I knew that they were thanking me for speaking with Paul in the manner that I had for the past months. It was three months since Paul conveyed to me that his father had just been diagnosed with a terminal illness. Even though he had said that his father had no more than a year, I knew it was now.

The next day on Sunday morning, Paul texted me that his father had died the morning prior, Saturday morning. I offered my sincere condolences of course. Then I said, "I know. I found the tenth dime."

One of the most difficult things we experience in this human life is unhealthy comparison. Many of our difficulties on earth stem from our comparing ourselves or what is occurring in our life to something other than what we are or what we have.

CHAPTER 33

Our Memory and Crossing Over

I had learned a great deal in my journey. I learned that we are born with many connectors in our brains. Over the first five years of our life, most of them disappear. We learn early on which ones are necessary for our human existence. They approximate 10% of our connectors. Those are the ones that we funnel all of our energy to. The other ones fall by the wayside. Our amazing brains and bodies learn to adapt to the world in which we live, so that we can survive and flourish. This explains why children seem to be most in tune with the other side. As we grow older, we learn to spend our resources on being able to navigate our human life, so our spiritual connections dissipate in most cases.

I learned that we do not recall our past lives as a sort of defense mechanism. If we were able to recall or knew too much about our past lives or our life between human lives, we would be more apt to be distracted from our purpose. If we had agreed to something too difficult, we may give up or try to choose not to accomplish our purpose. You can imagine that if we knew what the purpose or mission of others or of our loved ones are, we might be persuaded to attempt to help them or to possibly even abort their mission. For example, if one knew that her spouse had decided to leave earth in his 50's to help her to grow through that pain. That would be torturous. Both partners would be so preoccupied with that soul decision, that it would effect and likely stunt both of the growth paths.

We are here to enjoy our lives and to accomplish our challenges. We are not here to be preoccupied with our purpose.

I learned that when we first cross over, we experience a life review. We experience every aspect of our life in this review. However, we experience it from the perspective of the person that we interacted with. We feel the feelings of joy that we provided to others, strangers, and our family from their perspective. So we feel what they felt. We understand the feelings that we caused for other people. We feel the feelings of sorrow that we caused to others, to strangers, and to our family. Then we ourselves are our own judge on Judgement Day. After feeling our life during the life review, we decide if we successfully accomplished our purposes. We decide where we should reside on the other side. We decide if we have advanced enough to have helped ourselves and our soul group to grow.

The other side is levels of light. Those who are horrible on earth decide themselves after feeling how they hurt others to reside in the lowest light realm. They reside in pitch darkness, with no glimpse of light. You can imagine an entire existence in perfect darkness would be torturous. Trying to elevate themselves from that very dark abyss is very difficult. Seeing their way out is very challenging. Prayers from other souls, whether on earth or on the other side can help these souls.

The highest level of light is all of our collective souls in their brightest light forms. This would be a place of deep and true euphoria. Each one of us decides upon return which level of light we should reside in until we may decide to return to earth. Our soul group also resides in our level of light. We are all actually beings of light and energy. That is how it is possible for one soul to be in many places at one time. So, if a father and husband passes on, he is able to visit his children and his wife simultaneously. He is light energy. Light is an omnipresent energy. Light can shine and exist in many spaces all at the same time.

One of the reasons that it is so wonderful on the other side is because we reside only with those at our level of light or our evolution level. There are not souls that are less or more evolved than us. Living with similar soul levels is easy and peaceful. You can imagine if you only lived on earth with people who were at the same level as you how much easier your life would be. Of course, it would also be more difficult to experience the challenges that we encounter here and therefore growth would not be as significant as possible. However, on the other side, there is no fear because souls of lower evolution levels are not there. There is nothing to be fearful about. There is no jealousy or feelings of inadequacy because souls of higher evolution levels are not there either. There is nothing to be jealous of. One of the most difficult things we experience in this human life is unhealthy comparison. We compare ourselves to others. We compare ourselves to ourselves at a younger age. We compare ourselves to the goals that we aspire to. This can be inspiring, but more often, it is detrimental. This need for comparison is not existent on the other side. Many of our difficulties on earth stem from us comparing ourselves or what is occurring in our life to something other than what we are or what we have.

Comparison is typically an unhealthy aspect of our human existence.

I also learned that we only take the percent of our soul to earth that we believe to be necessary to accomplish our tasks and goals while on earth. This is an important and difficult concept for us to appreciate. If our life on earth is particularly difficult, then we will take with us a higher percent of our soul, maybe all of it or 90% of it. If our life on earth is not too difficult, then we would only need to take a lesser percent, like maybe 70%. Whether we take a percent of our soul or our entire soul, we are always connected to the other side. So, whereas this seems like a drastic measure to a human, the decision to take a portion of your soul is really not that significant a decision for a soul.

Someone who is going to die violently may take a large percent of their soul and will also have some repair time to rejuvenate their energy while back on the other side. Passing due to violence is interesting because when it is someone's chosen time to go back, they will actually leave their soul before the actual human form or body dies. They will not experience what we would think in terms of excessive pain in their last moments.

We cannot understand this fully because we all have felt deep physical pain at one time or another. It may have been from illness or from an injury. When we think of anyone crossing back due to a violent act, we can only imagine that they physically felt something far worse than the physical pain that we felt during our injury or illness. It is simply our only frame of reference. Additionally, we have all felt hopelessness and desperation at one time or another. So, if someone is a victim of a violent act, we can only imagine that they emotionally felt something far worse than the emotional pain that we felt during our times of sorrow and despair. It is simply our only frame of reference. And there are souls that endure violent acts of abuse, yet they don't pass. In those cases, they can convey their horrible pain and emotional abuse. So, with all of this information, we understandably know that anyone that died from an act of violence must have suffered tremendously. This will haunt their loved ones. However, when a soul knows that it is their time to cross back, their soul will extricate from their body during the violent acts and begin the transition back to the other side prior to their actual earthly death. So the pain in their final moments is not what we may imagine it to be. For those with a loved one that died violently, this can provide some semblance of comfort. They did not physically suffer as much as we might imagine in their very final moments. Remember, we have already chosen how and when we will return to the other side. So, once a soul recognizes that what is occurring is what they sort of agreed to, they will quickly transition out of their body and remove themselves from the painful situation.

I once met a woman at a business conference. We happened to be seated next to one another for the lunch break. The topic of children came up and she disclosed to me that her 23-year-old son had died years ago in a single car crash. She said it was a mystery because his truck veered off the road on a perfectly partly sunny afternoon. No substance use, no slick spot on the road, no excessive sun glare, no bad weather and nothing seemingly to cause the accident. She, of course, was horribly distraught. She also was a daily meditator. She told me that one evening during her meditation about three years after the accident, her son spoke to her. She said his voice was crystal clear and he said three sentences, "The accident did not cause my soul to leave my body. My soul leaving my body caused the accident. It was my time." She said that she took comfort in that.

I was astonished. A young healthy fellow dying in a single car crash and speaking these specific words about his crossing. I said to her that this was a pearl of information coming from someone who had already crossed. It made me think about fatal single person accidents in an entirely different way. I don't think there would ever be a way to think of single person accidents in this way if it was not for someone who died as a result of one letting us know after he died how it had occurred. The accident did not cause his death. His soul left his body first and then subsequently the fatal accident occurred. This is fascinating information.

As we grow older, we learn to spend our resources on being able to navigate our human life, so our spiritual connections dissipate in most cases.

CHAPTER 34

Melissa

My niece, Melissa, was born with cancer. It was not detected until she was one year old. By then, it had spread to many of her organs. The wonderful physicians that cared for her said that the chance of Melissa surviving to five years of age was less than 15%. The year following her diagnosis included aggressive treatments. Her tiny body underwent surgeries, radiation therapy treatments, and chemotherapy. She did survive. She is incredible and she surpassed all of the odds. She survived past five years of age. She lived until she was 32 years of age.

Interspersed with her doctors' appointments, she had a wonderful life. Although her body was special needs due to the treatments, her personality was undeniable. She was in love with us, her family, and we were in love with her.

If you've ever had the blessing of having someone that is special needs in your circle of close family or friends, you know what I mean. She was honest, bubbly, strong-willed, and funny. She was unconditional love. Unfortunately, her final four years on earth were spent fighting for her life, as she had done at the beginning of her life here. She was the strongest person that I've ever met and will likely ever meet. Although her quality of life was tumultuous in the end, she still fought to stay alive. She taught me that no matter the circumstances, staying alive should be a priority. She passed over relatively peaceably in a local Hospice Inn. She was the closest person to me that died since I had learned about the afterlife.

During the late afternoon of the day that she passed, I was on my way to my in-laws' home. I had picked up my adult son, some food, and we were somberly driving there. On our way, my telephone, which was in my pocketbook in the back seat of my car, began to ring. I listened to it ringing. I turned to my son, who was in the front seat next to me and asked if it was my telephone or his. He said it was mine. I found it curious that it was not automatically coming through my car's speaker system, since my telephone was connected to my car via Bluetooth. I assumed that the connection had erroneously disconnected. I asked my son if he could reach my telephone in the back seat. He tried, but could not. We decided that I would wait until we got to our destination and I would check to see who had called at that time. The phone continued to ring unanswered for a couple of minutes. I found it curious that the message answering feature of my telephone was not picking up the call and instead it was ringing and ringing. I assumed the feature was disabled for some bizarre reason. We continued on our way.

When we arrived at my in-laws' house a few minutes later, I parked the car and immediately grabbed my pocketbook and my telephone. I wanted to see whose call I missed. Lo and behold, there was no missed call at all. I handed the telephone to my son figuring that possibly I was missing something. He searched. He also could find no missed call. We looked at one another. We both heard the telephone ringing and ringing. There was no denying that. It could not have come from anywhere else. It had been my telephone in the back seat of the car. I immediately thought of Melissa. I had heard that often signs come through during the first three days after a loved one crosses. Could she somehow have been ringing my phone? It was so soon after she passed though. I know that our loved ones are free of the physical encumbrances that they may have had during their final days. They are eager to convey to us that they are really still around. As the upcoming days passed,

I learned that this was the first of many great signs from my beautiful niece, Melissa!

After discovering no message on my telephone, the afternoon that Melissa passed, my son and I went into my in-laws' house. The energy was so very sad. We all felt such a deep feeling of loss, grief and sorrow. I cannot imagine how horrible it was for my sister-in-law and brother-in-law. We laid out the dinner that we brought. We all picked a bit, but nobody had much of an appetite. My son and I told the story about the mysterious telephone call in the car earlier. A bit after that, the house telephone rang. My sister-in-law looked at the phone. The telephone screen indicated that the call was coming from Ocean City, Maryland. She picked up the phone. There was nobody on the other end. After several times of Laura saying, "Hello" and her receiving no answer, they got disconnected. She hung up and said, "Melissa's at the beach."

The following day, my daughter was driving to visit my parents. She came back home after just a few minutes. She was excited. She had turned on the radio. The station that she turned on was playing one of Melissa's favorite songs, played by Melissa's favorite band, the Backstreet Boys. This band had not released a recent song in years. The song playing on the radio was an old one and one of Melissa's favorite ones. My daughter said that it was the first song when she turned the radio on. But then, the volume went up loud on its own without Diana touching the volume buttons! Diana lowered the volume and then the volume did it again! The volume increased without Diana touching the volume button. Diana was positive that it was a sign from Melissa. I agreed. Melissa was seven years older than Diana. Melissa was there when Diana was a baby, when Diana was a toddler, when Diana was a teenager and now that Diana was an adult. Melissa worshipped Diana. Diana loves Melissa with all of her heart. Of course, Melissa would make sure Diana knew that she was ok, that her soul was alive and well.

My daughter redirected. Instead of continuing to drive to my parents' house, she came home to let me know what had happened. We were both marveling in what had happened. After calming down, Diana decided to start her trip to my parents once again. I decided that I would join her for the visit. We headed back to my parents, this time in my car, instead of Diana's car. We did not turn on the radio. We were just chatting on our way there. About five minutes into our trip, there was a lull in our conversation. I said, "Wouldn't it be amazing if we turned on the radio now and the Backstreet Boys were playing?" We both chuckled. So that is what I did. I turned on the radio. And lo and behold, it was the very beginning of a song by the

Backstreet Boys! We looked at each other in disbelief and excitement. We thanked Melissa out loud.

A few months after Melissa died, I was inspired by a book that the nationally-renowned medium, Laura Lynne Jackson, had written. The medium encouraged our giving the other side difficult and prescriptive things to show us that they are still around. The medium said it should be something so unique that we would not be able to discount it as anything other than an obvious sign. I decided to ask Melissa to show me a zebra.

I remembered from my first encounter with Josephine G. at the start of my afterlife journey, that it may take up to two weeks for our loved ones to present us with our specifically requested sign. So over the course of the upcoming days, I was hopeful that I would see a zebra. I did see some black and white striped items, but not a zebra. Not just yet. Then on the 13th day after I asked for the zebra sign, I was flying to Florida for a vacation weekend. I was in a window seat. A young fellow sat in the middle seat. He struck up a conversation with the man in the aisle seat of our row. I overheard that the 19-year-old was on his way home to Florida from South Africa. And yes, he had been on several safaris. He went on and on about lions, elephants, panthers, leopards and rhinos. He mentioned each of these animals many times as he spoke for about a half hour. He had pictures on his telephone of all of these wonderful animals. I was looking over his shoulder as he thumbed through his pictures. Then he mentioned that he also saw a giraffe and yes, he saw a zebra. He showed those pictures. I looked over his shoulder and saw his picture of a zebra. One mention, no more. But I knew it was for me! Thank you, Melissa!

CHAPTER 35

Immortality

So, I share my journey with you because I hope that it may help you to see what we experience while we are here on earth in a different way. I am hopeful that this new perspective may help you or someone to move through a difficult time in an easier way. Knowledge is the antidote to fear. Unfortunately, it does not eradicate grief. Losing someone that we love so dearly elicits a grief that is most difficult to work through. However the knowledge that there is a greater purpose, the knowledge that our loved ones are still very close to us, the knowledge that we will be with them again, and the knowledge that they chose to leave in the manner in which they passed may provide a modest amount of comfort.

I was quite motivated to assemble my knowledge and my journey in a format that may help someone. We are all on our own individual paths. "You believe in the afterlife, don't you?" my friend said incredulously. Back then, I was not sure if I believed. I had not really thought about it. Now though, yes, I believe. It is actually different from believing. It is not an intuition or a feeling or a belief really. It is just that I have learned, experienced and seen too much for there to be any explanation other than the existence of an afterlife. So, what is that — a convincing? Yes, I am convinced that we are all immortal.

ACKNOWLEDGMENTS

I sincerely want to thank my family and friends who allowed me to pitch my myriads of thoughts and decisions as I formed this book. Ralph Marinaccio, my husband, Diana Marinaccio, my daughter, Joseph Marinaccio, my son, Lynda Gennaro, my sister, my parents, and my in-laws. To have people in my life who love me and who I can trust fully and completely is such a blessing. It's impossible to thank you adequately for your support.

I also want to thank my close friends. Joann Lacey, Maria Peccia and Martha Stark have supported and encouraged me to write and to continue to write this book. Through the years, your positive attitudes and encouragement helped me to continue to bring this together.

I have friends and colleagues who were pivotal in bringing the final touches to the book. I want to thank Melissa Gould, Tom Gould, Karen Garvey and David F.

Wright. Finalizing this project was a bit overwhelming to me. You each had an important part in helping me to navigate the final steps. I want to thank Brian Ballweg also. He is the talented photographer who took my head shot.

After I wrote the book, I gathered the courage to ask Laura Lynne Jackson, Robert Hansen and Josephine Ghiringhelli to read it and to provide me with an endorsement if they were so inclined. I want to thank each of you for your part in my understanding of the afterlife, as well as your time to read my book and to provide your words of support and encouragement.

I must honor my mother-in-law, Lucille Marinaccio, and my uncle, Charles Gennaro. Their persistence after they died to help me to understand that there is an afterlife is nothing short of a miracle. They were determined people when they lived and it was evident after they crossed over as they patiently and methodically helped me to understand all of this. They conveyed the information to me in a slow and systematic manner, so I was able to appreciate each piece before they would convey the next grouping of information.

Lastly, I want to honor and thank three people who were alive when I began to learn about the afterlife, but who have crossed since then. They each played significant, yet different, roles in my life and development. Phran

Ginsberg, one of the founders of the Forever Family Foundation, Robin Murray, a co-volunteer with me at the Forever Family Foundation, and my beautiful and vivacious niece, Melissa.

Manufactured by Amazon.ca
Bolton, ON

43783709R00125